DEATH
AND
THE KING'S
HORSEMAN

WOLE SOYINKA

W. W. Norton & Company
New York   London

Reissued as a Norton paperback 2002

Library of Congress Cataloging-in-Publication Data
Soyinka, Wole.
    Death and the king's horseman.
    1. Elesin—Drama. 2. Nigeria—History—Drama.
I. Title
PR9387.9.S6D4 1976 822 75-42079
ISBN 0-393-04422-X
ISBN 0-393-04429-7
ISBN 0-393-32299-8 pbk.

Printed in the United States of America

W. W. Norton & Company, Inc.
500 Fifth Avenue, New York, N.Y. 10110
www.wwnorton.com

W. W. Norton & Company Ltd.
Castle House, 75/76 Wells Street, London W1T 3QT

    6 7 8 9 0

Dedicated
In Affectionate Greeting
to
My Father, Ayodele
who lately danced, and joined the Ancestors.

AUTHOR'S NOTE

This play is based on events which took place in Oyo, ancient
Yoruba city of Nigeria, in 1946. That year, the lives of Elesin
(Olori Elesin), his son, and the Colonial District Officer inter-
twined with the disastrous results set out in the play. The
changes I have made are in matters of detail, sequence and of
course characterisation. The action has also been set back two
or three years to while the war was still on, for minor reasons
of dramaturgy.

The factual account still exists in the archives of the British
Colonial Administration. It has already inspired a fine play in
Yoruba (Oba Wàjà) by Duro Ladipo. It has also misbegotten a
film by some German television company.

The bane of themes of this genre is that they are no sooner
employed creatively than they acquire the facile tag of 'clash
of cultures', a prejudicial label which, quite apart from its
frequent misapplication, presupposes a potential equality *in
every given situation* of the alien culture and the indigenous, on
the actual soil of the latter. (In the area of misapplication, the
overseas prize for illiteracy and mental conditioning undoubtedly
goes to the blurb-writer for the American edition of my novel
Season of Anomy who unblushingly declares that this work
portrays the 'clash between old values and new ways, between
western methods and African traditions'!) It is thanks to this
kind of perverse mentality that I find it necessary to caution
the would-be producer of this play against a sadly familiar
reductionist tendency, and to direct his vision instead to the
far more difficult and risky task of eliciting the play's threnodic
essence.

One of the more obvious alternative structures of the play
would be to make the District Officer the victim of a cruel
dilemma. This is not to my taste and it is not by chance that
I have avoided dialogue or situation which would encourage

this. No attempt should be made in production to suggest it. The Colonial Factor is an incident, a catalytic incident merely. The confrontation in the play is largely metaphysical, contained in the human vehicle which is Elesin and the universe of the Yoruba mind - the world of the living, the dead and the unborn, and the numinous passage which links all: transition. *Death and the King's Horseman* can be fully realised only through an evocation of music from the abyss of transition.

W.S.

DEATH
AND
THE KING'S
HORSEMAN

CHARACTERS

PRAISE-SINGER
ELESIN   Horseman of the King
IYALOJA   'Mother' of the market
SIMON PILKINGS   District Officer
JANE PILKINGS   his wife
SERJEANT AMUSA
JOSEPH   houseboy to the Pilkingses
BRIDE
H.R.H. THE PRINCE
THE RESIDENT
AIDE-DE-CAMP
OLUNDE   eldest son of Elesin

Drummers, Women, Young Girls, Dancers at the Ball

*The play should run without an interval. For rapid scene changes,
one adjustable outline set is very appropriate.*

Note to this edition

Certain Yoruba words which appear in italics in the text are
explained in a brief glossary at the back of the book.

1

A passage through a market in its closing stages. The stalls are being emptied, mats folded. A few women pass through on their way home, loaded with baskets. On a cloth-stand, bolts of cloth are taken down, display pieces folded and piled on a tray. ELESIN OBA enters along a passage before the market, pursued by his drummers and praise-singers. He is a man of enormous vitality, speaks, dances and sings with that infectious enjoyment of life which accompanies all his actions.

PRAISE-SINGER: Elesin o! Elesin Oba! Howu! What tryst is this the cockerel goes to keep with such haste that he must leave his tail behind?

ELESIN (slows down a bit, laughing): A tryst where the cockerel needs no adornment.

PRAISE-SINGER: O-oh, you hear that my companions? That's the way the world goes. Because the man approaches a brand-new bride he forgets the long faithful mother of his children.

ELESIN: When the horse sniffs the stable does he not strain at the bridle? The market is the long-suffering home of my spirit and the women are packing up to go. That Esu-harrassed day slipped into the stewpot while we feasted. We ate it up with the rest of the meat. I have neglected my women.

PRAISE-SINGER: We know all that. Still it's no reason for shedding your tail on this day of all days. I know the women will cover you in damask and *alari* but when the wind blows cold from behind, that's when the fowl knows his true friends.

ELESIN: Olohun-iyo!

PRAISE-SINGER: Are you sure there will be one like me on the other side?

ELESIN: Olohun-iyo!

PRAISE-SINGER: Far be it for me to belittle the dwellers of that place but, a man is either born to his art or he isn't. And I don't know for certain that you'll meet my father, so who is going to sing these deeds in accents that will pierce the deafness of the ancient ones. I have prepared my going - just tell me: Olohun-iyo, I need you on this journey and I shall be behind you.

ELESIN: You're like a jealous wife. Stay close to me, but only on this side. My fame, my honour are legacies to the living; stay behind and let the world sip its honey from your lips.

PRAISE-SINGER: Your name will be like the sweet berry a child places under his tongue to sweeten the passage of food. The world will never spit it out.

ELESIN: Come then. This market is my roost. When I come among the women I am a chicken with a hundred mothers. I become a monarch whose palace is built with tenderness and beauty.

PRAISE-SINGER: They love to spoil you but beware. The hands of women also weaken the unwary.

ELESIN: This night I'll lay my head upon their lap and go to sleep. This night I'll touch feet with their feet in a dance that is no longer of this earth. But the smell of their flesh, their sweat, the smell of indigo on their cloth, this is the last air I wish to breathe as I go to meet my great forebears.

PRAISE-SINGER: In their time the world was never tilted from its groove, it shall not be in yours.

ELESIN: The gods have said No.

PRAISE-SINGER: In their time the great wars came and went, the little wars came and went; the white slavers came and went, they took away the heart of our race, they bore away the mind and muscle of our race. The city fell and was rebuilt; the city fell and our people trudged through mountain and forest to found a new home but - Elesin Oba do you hear me?

ELESIN: I hear your voice Olohun-iyo.

PRAISE-SINGER: Our world was never wrenched from its true course.

ELESIN: The gods have said No.

PRAISE-SINGER: There is only one home to the life of a river-mussel; there is only one home to the life of a tortoise; there is only one shell to the soul of man: there is only one world to the spirit of our race. If that world leaves its course and smashes on boulders of the great void, whose world will give us shelter?

ELESIN: It did not in the time of my forebears, it shall not in mine.

PRAISE-SINGER: The cockerel must not be seen without his feathers.

ELESIN: Nor will the Not-I bird be much longer without his nest.

PRAISE-SINGER (stopped in his lyric stride): The Not-I bird, Elesin?

ELESIN: I said, the Not-I bird.

PRAISE-SINGER: All respect to our elders but, is there really such a bird?

ELESIN: What! Could it be that he failed to knock on your door?

PRAISE-SINGER (smiling): Elesin's riddles are not merely the nut in the kernel that breaks human teeth; he also buries the kernel in hot embers and dares a man's fingers to draw it out.

ELESIN: I am sure he called on you, Olohun-iyo. Did you hide in the loft and push out the servant to tell him you were out?

(ELESIN executes a brief, half-taunting dance. The drummer moves in and draws a rhythm out of his steps. ELESIN dances towards the market-place as he chants the story of the Not-I bird, his voice changing dexterously to mimic his characters. He performs like a born raconteur, infecting his retinue with his humour and energy. More women arrive during his recital, including IYALOJA.)

> Death came calling.
> Who does not know his rasp of reeds?
> A twilight whisper in the leaves before
> The great araba falls? Did you hear it?
> Not I! swears the farmer. He snaps
> His fingers round his head, abandons
> A hard-worn harvest and begins

A rapid dialogue with his legs.

'Not I,' shouts the fearless hunter, 'but -
It's getting dark, and this night-lamp
Has leaked out all its oil. I think
It's best to go home and resume my hunt
Another day.' But now he pauses, suddenly
Lets out a wail: 'Oh foolish mouth, calling
Down a curse on your own head! Your lamp
Has leaked out all its oil, has it?'
Forwards or backwards now he dare not move.
To search for leaves and make *etutu*
On that spot? Or race home to the safety
Of his hearth? Ten market-days have passed
My friends, and still he's rooted there
Rigid as the plinth of Orayan.

The mouth of the courtesan barely
Opened wide enough to take a ha'penny *robo*
When she wailed: 'Not I.' All dressed she was
To call upon my friend the Chief Tax Officer.
But now she sends her go-between instead:
'Tell him I'm ill: my period has come suddenly
But not - I hope - my time.'

Why is the pupil crying?
His hapless head was made to taste
The knuckles of my friend the Mallam:
'If you were then reciting the Koran
Would you have ears for idle noises
Darkening the trees, you child of ill omen?'
He shuts down school before its time
Runs home and rings himself with amulets.

And take my good kinsman Ifawomi.
His hands were like a carver's, strong
And true. I saw them
Tremble like wet wings of a fowl
One day he cast his time-smoothed *opele*
Across the divination board. And all because
The suppliant looked him in the eye and asked,
'Did you hear that whisper in the leaves?'
'Not I,' was his reply; 'perhaps I'm growing deaf
Good-day.' And Ifa spoke no more that day
The priest locked fast his doors,

Sealed up his leaking roof - but wait!
This sudden care was not for Fawomi
But for Osanyin, courier-bird of Ifa's
Heart of wisdom. I did not know a kite
Was hovering in the sky
And Ifa now a twittering chicken in
The brood of Fawomi the Mother Hen.

Ah, but I must not forget my evening
Courier from the abundant palm, whose groan
Became Not I, as he constipated down
A wayside bush. He wonders if Elegbara
Has tricked his buttocks to discharge
Against a sacred grove. Hear him
Mutter spells to ward off penalties
For an abomination he did not intend.
If any here
Stumbles on a gourd of wine, fermenting
Near the road, and nearby hears a stream
Of spells issuing from a crouching form.
Brother to a *sigidi*, bring home my wine,
Tell my tapper I have ejected
Fear from home and farm. Assure him,
All is well.

PRAISE-SINGER: In your time we do not doubt the peace of
    farmstead and home, the peace of road and hearth, we do not
    doubt the peace of the forest.

ELESIN: There was fear in the forest too.
Not-I was lately heard even in the lair
Of beasts. The hyena cackled loud Not I,
The civet twitched his fiery tail and glared:
Not I. Not-I became the answering-name
Of the restless bird, that little one
Whom Death found nesting in the leaves
When whisper of his coming ran
Before him on the wind. Not-I
Has long abandoned home. This same dawn
I heard him twitter in the gods' abode.
Ah, companions of this living world
What a thing this is, that even those
We call immortal
Should fear to die.

13

IYALOJA:	But you, husband of multitudes?
ELESIN:	I, when that Not-I bird perched Upon my roof, bade him seek his nest again, Safe, without care or fear. I unrolled My welcome mat for him to see. Not-I Flew happily away, you'll hear his voice No more in this lifetime - You all know What I am.
PRAISE-SINGER:	That rock which turns its open lodes Into the path of lightning. A gay Thoroughbred whose stride disdains To falter though an adder reared Suddenly in his path.
ELESIN:	My rein is loosened. I am master of my Fate. When the hour comes Watch me dance along the narrowing path Glazed by the soles of my great precursors. My soul is eager. I shall not turn aside.
WOMEN:	You will not delay?
ELESIN:	Where the storm pleases, and when, it directs The giants of the forest. When friendship summons Is when the true comrade goes.
WOMEN:	Nothing will hold you back?
ELESIN:	Nothing. What! Has no one told you yet? I go to keep my friend and master company. Who says the mouth does not believe in 'No, I have chewed all that before?' I say I have. The world is not a constant honey-pot. Where I found little I made do with little. Where there was plenty I gorged myself. My master's hands and mine have always Dipped together and, home or sacred feast, The bowl was beaten bronze, the meats So succulent our teeth accused us of neglect. We shared the choicest of the season's Harvest of yams. How my friend would read Desire in my eyes before I knew the cause - However rare, however precious, it was mine.

WOMEN:	The town, the very land was yours.
ELESIN:	The world was mine. Our joint hands Raised houseposts of trust that withstood The siege of envy and the termites of time. But the twilight hour brings bats and rodents - Shall I yield them cause to foul the rafters?
PRAISE-SINGER:	Elesin Oba! Are you not that man who Looked out of doors that stormy day The god of luck limped by, drenched To the very lice that held His rags together? You took pity upon His sores and wished him fortune. Fortune was footloose this dawn, he replied, Till you trapped him in a heartfelt wish That now returns to you. Elesin Oba! I say you are that man who Chanced upon the calabash of honour You thought it was palm wine and Drained its contents to the final drop.
ELESIN:	Life has an end. A life that will outlive Fame and friendship begs another name. What elder takes his tongue to his plate, Licks it clean of every crumb? He will encounter Silence when he calls on children to fulfill The smallest errand! Life is honour. It ends when honour ends.
WOMEN:	We know you for a man of honour.

ELESIN: Stop! Enough of that!

WOMEN (puzzled, they whisper among themselves, turning mostly to IYALOJA): What is it? Did we say something to give offence? Have we slighted him in some way?

ELESIN: Enough of that sound I say. Let me hear no more in that vein. I've heard enough.

IYALOJA: We must have said something wrong. (Comes forward a little.) Elesin Oba, we ask forgiveness before you speak.

ELESIN: I am bitterly offended.

IYALOJA: Our unworthiness has betrayed us. All we can do is ask your forgiveness. Correct us like a kind father.

ELESIN: This day of all days . . .

IYALOJA: It does not bear thinking. If we offend you now we have mortified the gods. We offend heaven itself. Father of us all, tell us where we went astray. (She kneels, the other women follow.)

ELESIN:
Are you not ashamed? Even a tear-veiled
Eye preserves its function of sight.
Because my mind was raised to horizons
Even the boldest man lowers his gaze
In thinking of, must my body here
Be taken for a vagrant's?

IYALOJA: Horseman of the King, I am more baffled than ever.

PRAISE-SINGER: The strictest father unbends his brow when the child is penitent, Elesin. When time is short, we do not spend it prolonging the riddle. Their shoulders are bowed with the weight of fear lest they have marred your day beyond repair. Speak now in plain words and let us pursue the ailment to the home of remedies.

ELESIN:
Words are cheap. 'We know you for
A man of honour.' Well tell me, is this how
A man of honour should be seen?
Are these not the same clothes in which
I came among you a full half-hour ago?

(He roars with laughter and the women, relieved, rise and rush into stalls to fetch rich cloths.)

WOMAN: The gods are kind. A fault soon remedied is soon forgiven. Elesin Oba, even as we match our words with deed, let your heart forgive us completely.

ELESIN:
You who are breath and giver of my being
How shall I dare refuse you forgiveness
Even if the offence were real.

IYALOJA (dancing round him. Sings):
He forgives us. He forgives us.
What a fearful thing it is when
The voyager sets forth
But a curse remains behind.

WOMEN:	For a while we truly feared Our hands had wrenched the world adrift In emptiness.
IYALOJA:	Richly, richly, robe him richly The cloth of honour is *alari* *Sanyan* is the band of friendship Boa-skin makes slippers of esteem
WOMEN:	For a while we truly feared Our hands had wrenched the world adrift In emptiness.
PRAISE-SINGER:	He who must, must voyage forth The world will not roll backwards It is he who must, with one Great gesture overtake the world.
WOMEN:	For a while we truly feared Our hands had wrenched the world In emptiness.
PRAISE-SINGER:	The gourd you bear is not for shirking. The gourd is not for setting down At the first crossroad or wayside grove. Only one river may know its contents
WOMEN:	We shall all meet at the great market We shall all meet at the great market He who goes early takes the best bargains But we shall meet, and resume our banter.

(ELESIN stands resplendent in rich clothes, cap, shawl, etc. His sash is of a bright red *alari* cloth. The women dance round him. Suddenly, his attention is caught by an object off-stage.)

ELESIN:	The world I know is good.
WOMEN:	We know you'll leave it so.
ELESIN:	The world I know is the bounty Of hives after bees have swarmed. No goodness teems with such open hands Even in the dreams of deities.
WOMEN:	And we know you'll leave it so.
ELESIN:	I was born to keep it so. A hive

Is never known to wander. An anthill
Does not desert its roots. We cannot see
The still great womb of the world -
No man beholds his mother's womb -
Yet who denies it's there? Coiled
To the navel of the world is that
Endless cord that links us all
To the great origin. If I lose my way
The trailing cord will bring me to the roots.

WOMEN   The world is in your hands.

(The earlier distraction, a beautiful young girl, comes along the
passage through which ELESIN first made his entry.)

ELESIN: I embrace it. And let me tell you, women -
I like this farewell that the world designed,
Unless my eyes deceive me, unless
We are already parted, the world and I,
And all that breeds desire is lodged
Among our tireless ancestors. Tell me friends,
Am I still earthed in that beloved market
Of my youth? Or could it be my will
Has outleapt the conscious act and I have
          come
Among the great departed?

PRAISE-SINGER: Elesin-Oba why do your eyes roll like a bush-
rat who sees his fate like his father's spirit, mirrored in the
eye of a snake? And all these questions! You're standing on
the same earth you've always stood upon. This voice you hear
is mine, Oluhun-iyo, not that of an acolyte in heaven.

ELESIN: How can that be? In all my life
As Horseman of the King, the juiciest
Fruit on every tree was mine. I saw,
I touched, I wooed, rarely was the answer No.
The honour of my place, the veneration I
Received in the eye of man or woman
Prospered my suit and
Played havoc with my sleeping hours.
And they tell me my eyes were a hawk
In perpetual hunger. Split an iroko tree
In two, hide a woman's beauty in its heartwood
And seal it up again - Elesin, journeying by,

18

> Would make his camp beside that tree
> Of all the shades in the forest.

PRAISE-SINGER: Who would deny your reputation, snake-on-the-loose in dark passages of the market! Bed-bug who wages war on the mat and receives the thanks of the vanquished! When caught with his bride's own sister he protested - but I was only prostrating myself to her as becomes a grateful in-law. Hunter who carries his powder-horn on the hips and fires crouching or standing! Warrior who never makes that excuse of the whining coward - but how can I go to battle without my trousers? - trouserless or shirtless it's all one to him. Oka-rearing-from-a-camouflage-of-leaves, before he strikes the victim is already prone! Once they told him, Howu, a stallion does not feed on the grass beneath him: he replied, true, but surely he can roll on it!

WOMEN: Ba-a-a-ba O!

PRAISE-SINGER: Ah, but listen yet. You know there is the leaf-knibbling grub and there is the cola-chewing beetle; the leaf-nibbling grub lives on the leaf, the cola-chewing beetle lives in the colanut. Don't we know what our man feeds on when we find him cocooned in a woman's wrapper?

ELESIN:
> Enough, enough, you all have cause
> To know me well. But, if you say this earth
> Is still the same as gave birth to those songs,
> Tell me who was that goddess through whose
> > lips
> I saw the ivory pebbles of Oya's river-bed.
> Iyaloja, who is she? I saw her enter
> Your stall; all your daughters I know well.
> No, not even Ogun-of-the-farm toiling
> Dawn till dusk on his tuber patch
> Not even Ogun with the finest hoe he ever
> Forged at the anvil could have shaped
> That rise of buttocks, not though he had
> The richest earth between his fingers.
> Her wrapper was no disguise
> For thighs whose ripples shamed the river's
> Coils around the hills of Ilesi. Her eyes
> Were new-laid eggs glowing in the dark.
> Her skin . . .

IYALOJA: Elesin Oba . . .

ELESIN: What! Where do you all say I am?

IYALOJA: Still among the living.

ELESIN: And that radiance which so suddenly
          Lit up this market I could boast
          I knew so well?

IYALOJA: Has one step already in her husband's home. She is
betrothed.

ELESIN (irritated): Why do you tell me that?

(IYALOJA falls silent. The women shuffle uneasily.)

IYALOJA: Not because we dare give you offence Elesin. Today
is your day and the whole world is yours. Still, even those
who leave town to make a new dwelling elsewhere like to be
remembered by what they leave behind.

ELESIN: Who does not seek to be remembered?
          Memory is Master of Death, the chink
          In his armour of conceit. I shall leave
          That which makes my going the sheerest
          Dream of an afternoon. Should voyagers
          Not travel light? Let the considerate traveller
          Shed, of his excessive load, all
          That may benefit the living.

WOMEN (relieved): Ah Elesin Oba, we knew you for a man of
honour.

ELESIN: Then honour me. I deserve a bed of honour to lie upon.

IYALOJA: The best is yours. We know you for a man of honour.
You are not one who eats and leaves nothing on his plate for
children. Did you not say it yourself? Not one who blights
the happiness of others for a moment's pleasure.

ELESIN: Who speaks of pleasure? O women, listen!
          Pleasure palls. Our acts should have meaning.
          The sap of the plantain never dries.
          You have seen the young shoot swelling
          Even as the parent stalk begins to wither.
          Women, let my going be likened to
          The twilight hour of the plantain.

WOMEN: What does he mean Iyaloja? This language is the

language of our elders, we do not fully grasp it.

IYALOJA: I dare not understand you yet Elesin.

ELESIN:
All you who stand before the spirit that dares
The opening of the last door of passage,
Dare to rid my going of regrets! My wish
Transcends the blotting out of thought
In one mere moment's tremor of the senses.
Do me credit. And do me honour.
I am girded for the route beyond
Burdens of waste and longing.
Then let me travel light. Let
Seed that will not serve the stomach
On the way remain behind. Let it take root
In the earth of my choice, in this earth
I leave behind.

IYALOJA (turns to women): The voice I hear is already touched
by the waiting fingers of our departed. I dare not refuse.

WOMAN: But Iyaloja . . .

IYALOJA: The matter is no longer in our hands.

WOMAN: But she is betrothed to your own son. Tell him.

IYALOJA: My son's wish is mine. I did the asking for him, the
loss can be remedied. But who will remedy the blight of
closed hands on the day when all should be openness and
light? Tell him, you say! You wish that I burden him with
knowledge that will sour his wish and lay regrets on the last
moments of his mind. You pray to him who is your inter-
cessor to the other world - don't set this world adrift in
your own time; would you rather it was my hand whose
sacrilege wrenched it loose?

WOMAN: Not many men will brave the curse of a dispossessed
husband.

IYALOJA: Only the curses of the departed are to be feared.
The claims of one whose foot is on the threshold of their
abode surpasses even the claims of blood. It is impiety even
to place hindrances in their ways.

ELESIN:
What do my mothers say? Shall I step
Burdened into the unknown?

IYALOJA: Not we, but the very earth says No. The sap in the

plantain does not dry. Let grain that will not feed the voyager at his passage drop here and take root as he steps beyond this earth and us. Oh you who fill the home from hearth to threshold with the voices of children, you who now bestride the hidden gulf and pause to draw the right foot across and into the resting-home of the great forebears, it is good that your loins be drained into the earth we know, that your last strength be ploughed back into the womb that gave you being.

PRAISE-SINGER: Iyaloja, mother of multitudes in the teeming market of the world, how your wisdom transfigures you!

IYALOJA (smiling broadly, completely reconciled): Elesin, even at the narrow end of the passage I know you will look back and sigh a last regret for the flesh that flashed past your spirit in flight. You always had a restless eye. Your choice has my blessing. (To the women.) Take the good news to our daughter and make her ready. (Some women go off.)

ELESIN: Your eyes were clouded at first.

IYALOJA: Not for long. It is those who stand at the gateway of the great change to whose cry we must pay heed. And then, think of this - it makes the mind tremble. The fruit of such a union is rare. It will be neither of this world nor of the next. Nor of the one behind us. As if the timelessness of the ancestor world and the unborn have joined spirits to wring an issue of the elusive being of passage . . . Elesin!

ELESIN: I am here. What is it?

IYALOJA: Did you hear all I said just now?

ELESIN: Yes.

IYALOJA: The living must eat and drink. When the moment comes, don't turn the food to rodents' droppings in their mouth. Don't let them taste the ashes of the world when they step out at dawn to breathe the morning dew.

ELESIN: This doubt is unworthy of you Iyaloja.

IYALOJA: Eating the awusa nut is not so difficult as drinking water afterwards.

ELESIN: The waters of the bitter stream are honey to
                                a man
                           Whose tongue has savoured all.

22

IYALOJA: No one knows when the ants desert their home; they leave the mound intact. The swallow is never seen to peck holes in its nest when it is time to move with the season. There are always throngs of humanity behind the leave-taker. The rain should not come through the roof for them, the wind must not blow through the walls at night.

ELESIN: I refuse to take offence.

IYALOJA: You wish to travel light. Well, the earth is yours. But be sure the seed you leave in it attracts no curse.

ELESIN: You really mistake my person Iyaloja.

IYALOJA: I said nothing. Now we must go prepare your bridal chamber. Then these same hands will lay your shrouds.

ELESIN (exasperated): Must you be so blunt? (Recovers.) Well, weave your shrouds, but let the fingers of my bride seal my eyelids with earth and wash my body.

IYALOJA: Prepare yourself Elesin.

(She gets up to leave. At that moment the women return, leading the BRIDE. ELESIN's face glows with pleasure. He flicks the sleeves of his agbada with renewed confidence and steps forward to meet the group. As the girl kneels before IYALOJA, lights fade out on the scene.)

2

The verandah of the District Officer's bungalow. A tango is playing from an old hand-cranked gramophone and, glimpsed through the wide windows and doors which open onto the fore-stage verandah are the shapes of SIMON PILKINGS and his wife, JANE, tangoing in and out of shadows in the living-room. They are wearing what is immediately apparent as some form of fancy-dress. The dance goes on for some moments and then the figure of a 'Native Administration' policeman emerges and climbs up the steps onto the verandah. He peeps through and observes the dancing couple, reacting with what is obviously a long-standing bewilderment. He stiffens suddenly, his expression changes to one of disbelief and horror. In his excitement he upsets a flower-pot and attracts the attention of the couple. They stop dancing.

PILKINGS: Is there anyone out there?

JANE: I'll turn off the gramophone.

PILKINGS (approaching the verandah): I'm sure I heard something fall over. (The constable retreats slowly, open-mouthed as PILKINGS approaches the verandah.) Oh it's you Amusa. Why didn't you just knock instead of knocking things over?

AMUSA (stammers badly and points a shaky finger at his dress): Mista Pirinkin . . . Mista Pirinkin . . .

PILKINGS: What is the matter with you?

JANE (emerging): Who is it dear? Oh, Amusa . . .

PILKINGS: Yes it's Amusa, and acting most strangely.

AMUSA (his attention now transferred to MRS PILKINGS): Mammadam . . . you too!

PILKINGS: What the hell is the matter with you man!

JANE: Your costume darling. Our fancy dress.

PILKINGS: Oh hell, I'd forgotten all about that. (Lifts the face mask over his head showing his face. His wife follows suit.)

JANE: I think you've shocked his big pagan heart bless him.

PILKINGS: Nonsense, he's a Moslem. Come on Amusa, you don't believe in all this nonsense do you? I thought you were a good Moslem.

AMUSA: Mista Pirinkin, I beg you sir, what you think you do with that dress? It belong to dead cult, not for human being.

PILKINGS: Oh Amusa, what a let down you are. I swear by you at the club you know - thank God for Amusa, he doesn't believe in any mumbo-jumbo. And now look at you!

AMUSA: Mista Pirinkin, I beg you, take it off. Is not good for man like you to touch that cloth.

PILKINGS: Well, I've got it on. And what's more Jane and I have bet on it we're taking first prize at the ball. Now, if you can just pull yourself together and tell me what you wanted to see me about . . .

AMUSA: Sir, I cannot talk this matter to you in that dress. I no fit.

PILKINGS: What's that rubbish again?

JANE: He is dead earnest too Simon. I think you'll have to handle this delicately.

PILKINGS: Delicately my . . . ! Look here Amusa, I think this little joke has gone far enough hm? Let's have some sense. You seem to forget that you are a police officer in the service of His Majesty's Government. I order you to report your business at once or face disciplinary action.

AMUSA: Sir, it is a matter of death. How can man talk against death to person in uniform of death? Is like talking against government to person in uniform of police. Please sir, I go and come back.

PILKINGS (roars): Now! (AMUSA switches his gaze to the ceiling suddenly, remains mute.)

JANE: Oh Amusa, what is there to be scared of in the costume? You saw it confiscated last month from those *egungun* men who were creating trouble in town. You helped arrest the cult leaders yourself - if the juju didn't harm you at the time how could it possibly harm you now? And merely by looking at it?

AMUSA (without looking down): Madam, I arrrest the ring-leaders who make trouble but me I no touch *egungun*. That *egungun* inself, I no touch. And I no abuse 'am. I arrest ring-leader but I treat *egungun* with respect.

PILKINGS: It's hopeless. We'll merely end up missing the best part of the ball. When they get this way there is nothing you can do. It's simply hammering against a brick wall. Write your report or whatever it is on that pad Amusa and take yourself out of here. Come on Jane. We only upset his delicate sensi-bilities by remaining here.

(AMUSA waits for them to leave, then writes in the notebook, somewhat laboriously. Drumming from the direction of the town wells up. AMUSA listens, makes a movement as if he wants to recall PILKINGS but changes his mind. Completes his note and goes. A few moments later PILKINGS emerges, picks up the pad and reads.)

25

PILKINGS: Jane!

JANE (from the bedroom): Coming darling. Nearly ready.

PILKINGS: Never mind being ready, just listen to this.

JANE: What is it?

PILKINGS: Amusa's report. Listen. 'I have to report that it come to my information that one prominent chief, namely, the Elesin Oba, is to commit death tonight as a result of native custom. Because this is criminal offence I await further instruction at charge office. Sergeant Amusa.'

(JANE comes out onto the verandah while he is reading.)

JANE: Did I hear you say commit death?

PILKINGS: Obviously he means murder.

JANE: You mean a ritual murder?

PILKINGS: Must be. You think you've stamped it all out but it's always lurking under the surface somewhere.

JANE: Oh. Does it mean we are not getting to the ball at all?

PILKINGS: No-o. I'll have the man arrested. Everyone remotely involved. In any case there may be nothing to it. Just rumours.

JANE: Really? I thought you found Amusa's rumours generally reliable.

PILKINGS: That's true enough. But who knows what may have been giving him the scare lately. Look at his conduct tonight.

JANE (laughing): You have to admit he had his own peculiar logic. (Deepens her voice.) How can man talk against death to person in uniform of death? (Laughs.) Anyway, you can't go into the police station dressed like that.

PILKINGS: I'll send Joseph with instructions. Damn it, what a confounded nuisance!

JANE: But don't you think you should talk first to the man, Simon?

PILKINGS: Do you want to go to the ball or not?

JANE: Darling, why are you getting rattled? I was only trying to be intelligent. It seems hardly fair just to lock up a man - and a chief at that - simply on the er . . . what is that legal word again? - uncorroborated word of a sergeant.

26

PILKINGS: Well, that's easily decided. Joseph!

JOSEPH (from within): Yes master.

PILKINGS: You're quite right of course, I am getting rattled.
Probably the effect of those bloody drums. Do you hear how
they go on and on?

JANE: I wondered when you'd notice. Do you suppose it has
something to do with this affair?

PILKINGS: Who knows? They always find an excuse for making
a noise . . . (Thoughtfully.) Even so . . .

JANE: Yes Simon?

PILKINGS: It's different Jane. I don't think I've heard this
particular - sound - before. Something unsettling about it.

JANE: I thought all bush drumming sounded the same.

PILKINGS: Don't tease me now Jane. This may be serious.

JANE: I'm sorry. (Gets up and throws her arms around his neck.
Kisses him. The houseboy enters, retreats and knocks.)

PILKINGS (wearily): Oh, come in Joseph! I don't know where
you pick up all these elephantine notions of tact. Come over
here.

JOSEPH: Sir?

PILKINGS: Joseph, are you a christian or not?

JOSEPH: Yessir.

PILKINGS: Does seeing me in this outfit bother you?

JOSEPH: No sir, it has no power.

PILKINGS: Thank God for some sanity at last. Now Joseph,
answer me on the honour of a christian - what is supposed to
be going on in town tonight?

JOSEPH: Tonight sir? You mean that chief who is going to kill
himself?

PILKINGS: What?

JANE: What do you mean, kill himself?

PILKINGS: You do mean he is going to kill somebody don't you?

JOSEPH: No master. He will not kill anybody and no one will
kill him. He will simply die.

27

JANE: But why Joseph?

JOSEPH: It is native law and custom. The King die last month. Tonight is his burial. But before they can bury him, the Elesin must die so as to accompany him to heaven.

PILKINGS: I seem to be fated to clash more often with that man than with any of the other chiefs.

JOSEPH: He is the King's Chief Horseman.

PILKINGS (in a resigned way): I know.

JANE: Simon, what's the matter?

PILKINGS: It would have to be him!

JANE: Who is he?

PILKINGS: Don't you remember? He's that chief with whom I had a scrap some three or four years ago. I helped his son get to a medical school in England, remember? He fought tooth and nail to prevent it.

JANE: Oh now I remember. He was that very sensitive young man. What was his name again?

PILKINGS: Olunde. Haven't replied to his last letter come to think of it. The old pagan wanted him to stay and carry on some family tradition or the other. Honestly I couldn't understand the fuss he made. I literally had to help the boy escape from close confinement and load him onto the next boat. A most intelligent boy, really bright.

JANE: I rather thought he was much too sensitive you know. The kind of person you feel should be a poet munching rose petals in Bloomsbury.

PILKINGS: Well, he's going to make a first-class doctor. His mind is set on that. And as long as he wants my help he is welcome to it.

JANE (after a pause): Simon.

PILKINGS: Yes?

JANE: This boy, he was his eldest son wasn't he?

PILKINGS: I'm not sure. Who could tell with that old ram?

JANE: Do you know, Joseph?

JOSEPH: Oh yes madam. He was the eldest son. That's why

Elesin cursed master good and proper. The eldest son is not supposed to travel away from the land.

JANE (giggling): Is that true Simon? Did he really curse you good and proper?

PILKINGS: By all accounts I should be dead by now.

JOSEPH: Oh no, master is white man. And good christian. Black man juju can't touch master.

JANE: If he was his eldest, it means that he would be the Elesin to the next king. It's a family thing isn't it Joseph?

JOSEPH: Yes madam. And if this Elesin had died before the King, his eldest son must take his place.

JANE: That would explain why the old chief was so mad you took the boy away.

PILKINGS: Well it makes me all the more happy I did.

JANE: I wonder if he knew.

PILKINGS: Who? Oh, you mean Olunde?

JANE: Yes. Was that why he was so determined to get away? I wouldn't stay if I knew I was trapped in such a horrible custom.

PILKINGS (thoughtfully): No, I don't think he knew. At least he gave no indication. But you couldn't really tell with him. He was rather close you know, quite unlike most of them. Didn't give much away, not even to me.

JANE: Aren't they all rather close, Simon?

PILKINGS: These natives here? Good gracious. They'll open their mouths and yap with you about their family secrets before you can stop them. Only the other day . . .

JANE: But Simon, do they really give anything away? I mean, anything that really counts. This affair for instance, we didn't know they still practised that custom did we?

PILKINGS: Ye-e-es, I suppose you're right there. Sly, devious bastards.

JOSEPH (stiffly): Can I go now master? I have to clean the kitchen.

PILKINGS: What? Oh, you can go. Forgot you were still here.

(JOSEPH goes.)

JANE: Simon, you really must watch your language. Bastard isn't just a simple swear-word in these parts, you know.

PILKINGS: Look, just when did you become a social anthropologist, that's what I'd like to know.

JANE: I'm not claiming to know anything. I just happen to have overheard quarrels among the servants. That's how I know they consider it a smear.

PILKINGS: I thought the extended family system took care of all that. Elastic family, no bastards.

JANE (shrugs): Have it your own way.

(Awkward silence. The drumming increases in volume. JANE gets up suddenly, restless.)

That drumming Simon, do you think it might really be connected with this ritual? It's been going on all evening.

PILKINGS: Let's ask our native guide. Joseph! Just a minute Joseph. (JOSEPH re-enters.) What's the drumming about?

JOSEPH: I don't know master.

PILKINGS: What do you mean you don't know? It's only two years since your conversion. Don't tell me all that holy water nonsense also wiped out your tribal memory.

JOSEPH (visibly shocked): Master!

JANE: Now you've done it.

PILKINGS: What have I done now?

JANE: Never mind. Listen Joseph, just tell me this. Is that drumming connected with dying or anything of that nature?

JOSEPH: Madam, this is what I am trying to say: I am not sure. It sounds like the death of a great chief and then, it sounds like the wedding of a great chief. It really mix me up.

PILKINGS: Oh get back to the kitchen. A fat lot of help you are.

JOSEPH: Yes master. (Goes.)

JANE: Simon . . .

PILKINGS: Alright, alright. I'm in no mood for preaching.

JANE: It isn't my preaching you have to worry about, it's the preaching of the missionaries who preceded you here. When they make converts they really convert them. Calling holy

water nonsense to our Joseph is really like insulting the
Virgin Mary before a Roman Catholic. He's going to hand in
his notice tomorrow you mark my word.

PILKINGS: Now you're being ridiculous.

JANE: Am I? What are you willing to bet that tomorrow we are
going to be without a steward-boy? Did you see his face?

PILKINGS: I am more concerned about whether or not we will
be one native chief short by tomorrow. Christ! Just listen to
those drums. (He strides up and down, undecided.)

JANE (getting up): I'll change and make up some supper.

PILKINGS: What's that?

JANE: Simon, it's obvious we have to miss this ball.

PILKINGS: Nonsense. It's the first bit of real fun the European
club has managed to organise for over a year, I'm damned if
I'm going to miss it. And it is a rather special occasion.
Doesn't happen every day.

JANE: You know this business has to be stopped Simon. And
you are the only man who can do it.

PILKINGS: I don't have to stop anything. If they want to throw
themselves off the top of a cliff or poison themselves for the
sake of some barbaric custom what is that to me? If it were
ritual murder or something like that I'd be duty-bound to do
something. I can't keep an eye on all the potential suicides in
this province. And as for that man - believe me it's good
riddance.

JANE (laughs): I know you better than that Simon. You are
going to have to do something to stop it - after you've
finished blustering.

PILKINGS (shouts after her): And suppose after all it's only a
wedding. I'd look a proper fool if I interrupted a chief on his
honeymoon, wouldn't I? (Resumes his angry stride, slows
down.) Ah well, who can tell what those chiefs actually do
on their honeymoon anyway? (He takes up the pad and
scribbles rapidly on it.) Joseph! Joseph! Joseph! (Some
moments later JOSEPH puts in a sulky appearance.) Did you
hear me call you? Why the hell didn't you answer?

JOSEPH: I didn't hear master.

PILKINGS: You didn't hear me! How come you are here then?

JOSEPH (stubbornly): I didn't hear master.

PILKINGS (controls himself with an effort): We'll talk about it in the morning. I want you to take this note directly to Sergeant Amusa. You'll find him at the charge office. Get on your bicycle and race there with it. I expect you back in twenty minutes exactly. Twenty minutes, is that clear?

JOSEPH: Yes master. (Going.)

PILKINGS: Oh er . . . Joseph.

JOSEPH: Yes master?

PILKINGS (between gritted teeth): Er . . . forget what I said just now. The holy water is not nonsense. *I* was talking nonsense.

JOSEPH: Yes master. (Goes.)

JANE (pokes her head round the door): Have you found him?

PILKINGS: Found who?

JANE: Joseph. Weren't you shouting for him?

PILKINGS: Oh yes, he turned up finally.

JANE: You sounded desperate. What was it all about?

PILKINGS: Oh nothing. I just wanted to apologise to him. Assure him that the holy water isn't really nonsense.

JANE: Oh? And how did he take it?

PILKINGS: Who the hell gives a damn! I had a sudden vision of our Very Reverend Macfarlane drafting another letter of complaint to the Resident about my unchristian language towards his parishioners.

JANE: Oh I think he's given up on you by now.

PILKINGS: Don't be too sure. And anyway, I wanted to make sure Joseph didn't 'lose' my note on the way. He looked sufficiently full of the holy crusade to do some such thing.

JANE: If you've finished exaggerating, come and have something to eat.

PILKINGS: No, put it all way. We can still get to the ball.

JANE: Simon . . .

PILKINGS: Get your costume back on. Nothing to worry about.

I've instructed Amusa to arrest the man and lock him up.

JANE: But that station is hardly secure Simon. He'll soon get his friends to help him escape.

PILKINGS: A-ah, that's where I have out-thought you. I'm not having him put in the station cell. Amusa will bring him right here and lock him up in my study. And he'll stay with him till we get back. No one will dare come here to incite him to anything.

JANE: How clever of you darling. I'll get ready.

PILKINGS: Hey.

JANE: Yes darling.

PILKINGS: I have a surprise for you. I was going to keep it until we actually got to the ball.

JANE: What is it?

PILKINGS: You know the Prince is on a tour of the colonies don't you? Well, he docked in the capital only this morning but he is already at the Residency. He is going to grace the ball with his presence later tonight.

JANE: Simon! Not really.

PILKINGS: Yes he is. He's been invited to give away the prizes and he has agreed. You must admit old Engleton is the best Club Secretary we ever had. Quick off the mark that lad.

JANE: But how thrilling.

PILKINGS: The other provincials are going to be damned envious.

JANE: I wonder what he'll come as.

PILKINGS: Oh I don't know. As a coat-of-arms perhaps. Anyway it won't be anything to touch this.

JANE: Well that's lucky. If we are to be presented I won't have to start looking for a pair of gloves. It's all sewn on.

PILKINGS (laughing): Quite right. Trust a woman to think of that. Come on, let's get going.

JANE (rushing off): Won't be a second. (Stops.) Now I see why you've been so edgy all evening. I thought you weren't handling this affair with your usual brilliance - to begin with that is.

PILKINGS (his mood is much improved): Shut up woman and get your things on.

JANE: Alright boss, coming.

(PILKINGS suddenly begins to hum the tango to which they were dancing before. Starts to execute a few practice steps. Lights fade.)

3

A swelling, agitated hum of women's voices rises immediately in the background. The lights come on and we see the frontage of a converted cloth stall in the market. The floor leading up to the entrance is covered in rich velvets and woven cloth. The women come on stage, borne backwards by the determined progress of Sergeant AMUSA and his two constables who already have their batons out and use them as a pressure against the women. At the edge of the cloth-covered floor however the women take a determined stand and block all further progress of the men. They begin to tease them mercilessly.

AMUSA: I am tell you women for last time to commot my road. I am here on official business.

WOMAN: Official business you white man's eunuch? Official business is taking place where you want to go and it's a business you wouldn't understand.

WOMAN (makes a quick tug at the constable's baton): That doesn't fool anyone you know. It's the one you carry under your government knickers that counts. (She bends low as if to peep under the baggy shorts. The embarrassed constable quickly puts his knees together. The women roar.)

WOMAN: You mean there is nothing there at all?

WOMAN: Oh there was something. You know that handbell

which the whiteman uses to summon his servants . . . ?

AMUSA (he manages to preserve some dignity throughout): I hope you women know that interfering with officer in execution of his duty is criminal offence.

WOMAN: Interfere? He says we're interfering with him. You foolish man we're telling you there's nothing there to interfere with.

AMUSA: I am order you now to clear the road.

WOMAN: What road? The one your father built?

WOMAN: You are a Policeman not so? Then you know what they call trespassing in court. Or - (Pointing to the cloth-lined steps.) - do you think that kind of road is built for every kind of feet.

WOMAN: Go back and tell the white man who sent you to come himself.

AMUSA: If I go I will come back with reinforcement. And we will all return carrying weapons.

WOMAN: Oh, now I understand. Before they can put on those knickers the white man first cuts off their weapons.

WOMAN: What a cheek! You mean you come here to show power to women and you don't even have a weapon.

AMUSA: (shouting above the laughter): For the last time I warn you women to clear the road.

WOMAN: To where?

AMUSA: To that hut. I know he dey dere.

WOMAN: Who?

AMUSA: The chief who call himself Elesin Oba.

WOMAN: You ignorant man. It is not he who calls himself Elesin Oba, it is his blood that says it. As it called out to his father before him and will to his son after him. And that is in spite of everything your white man can do.

WOMAN: Is it not the same ocean that washes this land and the white man's land? Tell your white man he can hide our son away as long as he likes. When the time comes for him, the same ocean will bring him back.

AMUSA: The government say dat kin' ting must stop.

WOMAN: Who will stop it? You? Tonight our husband and father will prove himself greater than the laws of strangers.

AMUSA: I tell you nobody go prove anyting tonight or anytime. Is ignorant and criminal to prove dat kin' prove.

IYALOJA (entering, from the hut. She is accompanied by a group of young girls who have been attending the BRIDE): What is it Amusa? Why do you come here to disturb the happiness of others.

AMUSA: Madame Iyaloja, I glad you come. You know me. I no like trouble but duty is duty. I am here to arrest Elesin for criminal intent. Tell these women to stop obstructing me in the performance of my duty.

IYALOJA: And you? What gives you the right to obstruct our leader of men in the performance of his duty.

AMUSA: What kin' duty be dat one Iyaloja.

IYALOJA: What kin' duty? What kin' duty does a man have to his new bride?

AMUSA (bewildered, looks at the women and at the entrace to the hut): Iyaloja, is it wedding you call dis kin' ting?

IYALOJA: You have wives haven't you? Whatever the white man has done to you he hasn't stopped you having wives. And if he has, at least he is married. If you don't know what a marriage is, go and ask him to tell you.

AMUSA: This no to wedding.

IYALOJA: And ask him at the same time what he would have done if anyone had come to disturb him on his wedding night.

AMUSA: Iyaloja, I say dis no to wedding.

IYALOJA: You want to look inside the bridal chamber? You want to see for yourself how a man cuts the virgin knot?

AMUSA: Madam . . .

WOMAN: Perhaps his wives are still waiting for him to learn.

AMUSA: Iyaloja, make you tell dese women make den no insult me again. If I hear dat kin' indult once more . . .

GIRL (pushing her way through): You will do what?

GIRL: He's out of his mind. It's our mothers you're talking to, do you know that? Not to any illiterate villager you can bully and terrorise. How dare you intrude here anyway?

GIRL: What a cheek, what impertinence!

GIRL: You've treated them too gently. Now let them see what it is to tamper with the mothers of this market.

GIRLS: Your betters dare not enter the market when the women say no!

GIRL: Haven't you learnt that yet, you jester in khaki and starch?

IYALOJA: Daughters . . .

GIRL: No no Iyaloja, leave us to deal with him. He no longer knows his mother, we'll teach him.

(With a sudden movement they snatch the batons of the two constables. They begin to hem them in.)

GIRL: What next? We have your batons? What next? What are you going to do?

(With equally swift movements they knock off their hats.)

GIRL: Move if you dare. We have your hats, what will you do about it? Didn't the white man teach you to take off your hats before women?

IYALOJA: It's a wedding night. It's a night of joy for us. Peace . . .

GIRL: Not for him. Who asked him here?

GIRL: Does he dare go to the Residency without an invitation?

GIRL: Not even where the servants eat the left-overs.

GIRLS (in turn. In an 'English' accent): Well well it's Mister Amusa. Were you invited? (Play-acting to one another. The older women encourage them with their titters.)

- Your invitation card please?
- Who are you? Have we been introduced?
- And who did you say you were?
- Sorry, I didn't quite catch your name.
- May I take your hat?
- If you insist. May I take yours? (Exchanging the policeman's hats.)

- How very kind of you.
- Not at all. Won't you sit down?
- After you.
- Oh no.
- I insist.
- You're most gracious.
- And how do you find the place?
- The natives are alright.
- Friendly?
- Tractable.
- Not a teeny-weeny bit restless?
- Well, a teeny-weeny bit restless.
- One might even say, difficult?
- Indeed one might be tempted to say, difficult.
- But you do manage to cope?
- Yes indeed I do. I have a rather faithful ox called Amusa.
- He's loyal?
- Absolutely.
- Lay down his life for you what?
- Without a moment's thought.
- Had one like that once. Trust him with my life.
- Mostly of course they are liars.
- Never known a native tell the truth.
- Does it get rather close around here?
- It's mild for this time of the year.
- But the rains may still come.
- They are late this year aren't they?
- They are keeping African time.
- Ha ha ha ha
- Ha ha ha ha
- The humidity is what gets me.
- It used to be whisky.
- Ha ha ha ha
- Ha ha ha ha
- What's your handicap old chap?
- Is there racing by golly?
- Splendid golf course, you'll like it.
- I'm beginning to like it already.
- And a European club, exclusive.
- You've kept the flag flying.
- We do our best for the old country.
- It's a pleasure to serve.

- Another whisky old chap?
- You are indeed too too kind.
- Not at all sir. Where is that boy? (With a sudden bellow.) Sergeant!

AMUSA (snaps to attention): Yessir!

(The women collapse with laughter.)

GIRL: Take your men out of here.

AMUSA (realising the trick, he rages from loss of face): I'm give you warning . . .

GIRL: Alright then. Off with his knickers! (They surge slowly forward.)

IYALOJA: Daughters, please.

AMUSA (squaring himself for defence): The first woman wey touch me . . .

IYALOJA: My children, I beg of you . . .

GIRL: Then tell him to leave this market. This is the home of our mothers. We don't want the eater of white left-overs at the feast their hands have prepared.

IYALOJA: You heard them Amusa. You had better go.

GIRLS: Now!

AMUSA (commencing his retreat): We dey go now, but make you no say we no warn you.

GIRL: Now!

GIRL: Before we read the riot act - you should know all about that.

AMUSA: Make we go. (They depart, more precipitately.)

(The women strike their palms across in the gesture of wonder.)

WOMEN: Do they teach you all that at school?

WOMAN: And to think I nearly kept Apinke away from the place.

WOMAN: Did you hear them? Did you see how they mimicked the white man?

WOMAN: The voices exactly. Hey, there are wonders in this world!

IYALOJA: Well, our elders have said it: Dada may be weak, but he has a younger sibling who is truly fearless.

WOMAN: The next time the white man shows his face in this market I will set Wuraola on his tail.

(A woman bursts into song and dance of euphoria - 'Tani l'awa o l'ogbeja? Kayi! A l'ogbeja. Omo Kekere l'ogbeja.'* The rest of the women join in, some placing the girls on their back like infants, other dancing round them. The dance becomes general, mounting in excitement. ELESIN appears, in wrapper only. In his hands a white velvet cloth folded loosely as if it held some delicate object. He cries out.)

ELESIN: Oh you mothers of beautiful brides! (The dancing stops. They turn and see him, and the object in his hands. IYALOJA approaches and gently takes the cloth from him.) Take it. It is no mere virgin stain, but the union of life and the seeds of passage. My vital flow, the last from this flesh is intermingled with the promise of future life. All is prepared. Listen! (A steady drum-beat from the distance.) Yes. It is nearly time. The King's dog has been killed. The King's favourite horse is about to follow his master. My brother chiefs know their task and perform it well. (He listens again.)

(The BRIDE emerges, stands shyly by the door. He turns to her.)

Our marriage is not yet wholly fulfilled. When earth and passage wed, the consummation is complete only when there are grains of earth on the eyelids of passage. Stay by me till then. My faithful drummers, do me your last service. This is where I have chosen to do my leave-taking, in this heart of life, this hive which contains the swarm of the world in its small compass. This is where I have known love and laughter away from the palace. Even the richest food cloys when eaten days on end; in the market, nothing every cloys. Listen. (They listen to the drums.) They have begun to seek out the heart of the King's favourite horse. Soon it will ride in its bolt of raffia with the dog at its feet. Together they will ride on the shoulders of the King's grooms through the pulse centres of the town. They know it is here I shall await them. I have told them. (His eyes appear to cloud. He passes his

*'Who says we haven't a defender? Silence! We have our defenders. Little children are our champions'

40

hand over them as if to clear his sight. He gives a faint smile.)
It promises well; just then I felt my spirit's eagerness. The
kite makes for wide spaces and the wind creeps up behind its
tail; can the kite say less than - thank you, the quicker the
better? But wait a while my spirit. Wait. Wait for the coming
of the courier of the King. Do you know friends, the horse is
born to this one destiny, to bear the burden that is man upon
its back. Except for this night, this night alone when the
spotless stallion will ride in triumph on the back of man. In
the time of my father I witnessed the strange sight. Perhaps
tonight also I shall see it for the last time. If they arrive
before the drums beat for me, I shall tell him to let the
Alafin know I follow swiftly. If they come after the drums
have sounded, why then, all is well for I have gone ahead.
Our spirits shall fall in step along the great passage. (He
listens to the drums. He seems again to be falling into a state
of semi-hypnosis; his eyes scan the sky but it is in a kind of
daze. His voice is a little breathless.) The moon has fed, a
glow from its full stomach fills the sky and air, but I cannot
tell where is that gateway through which I must pass. My
faithful friends, let our feet touch together this last time,
lead me into the other market with sounds that cover my
skin with down yet make my limbs strike earth like a
thoroughbred. Dear mothers, let me dance into the passage
even as I have lived beneath your roofs. (He comes down
progressively among them. They make away for him, the
drummers playing. His dance is one of solemn, regal motions,
each gesture of the body is made with a solemn finality. The
women join him, their steps a somewhat more fluid version
of his. Beneath the PRAISE-SINGER's exhortations the
women dirge 'Alę lę lę, awo mi lọ'.)

PRAISE-SINGER:	Elesin Alafin, can you hear my voice?
ELESIN:	Faintly, my friend, faintly.
PRAISE-SINGER:	Elesin Alafin, can you hear my call?
ELSIN:	Faintly my king, faintly.
PRAISE-SINGER:	Is your memory sound Elesin? Shall my voice be a blade of grass and Tickle the armpit of the past?
ELESIN:	My memory needs no prodding but What do you wish to say to me?

PRAISE-SINGER: Only what has been spoken. Only what
        concerns
    The dying wish of the father of all.

ELESIN: It is buried like seed-yam in my mind
    This is the season of quick rains, the harvest
    Is this moment due for gathering.

PRAISE-SINGER: If you cannot come, I said, swear
    You'll tell my favourite horse. I shall
    Ride on through the gates alone.

ELESIN: Elesin's message will be read
    Only when his loyal heart no longer beats.

PRAISE-SINGER: If you cannot come Elesin, tell my dog.
    I cannot stay the keeper too long
    At the gate.

ELESIN: A dog does not outrun the hand
    That feeds it meat. A horse that throws its
        rider
    Slows down to a stop. Elesin Alafin
    Trusts no beasts with messages between
    A king and his companion.

PRAISE-SINGER: If you get lost my dog will track
    The hidden path to me.

ELESIN: The seven-way crossroads confuses
    Only the stranger. The Horseman of the King
    Was born in the recesses of the house.

PRAISE-SINGER: I know the wickedness of men. If there is
    Weight on the loose end of your sash, such
        weight
    As no mere man can shift; if your sash is
        earthed
    By evil minds who mean to part us at the
        last . . .

ELESIN: My sash is of the deep purple *alari*;
    It is no tethering-rope. The elephant
    Trails no tethering-rope; that king
    Is not yet crowned who will peg an elephant -
    Not even you my friend and King.

PRAISE-SINGER: And yet this fear will not depart from me

	The darkness of this new abode is deep -
	Will your human eyes suffice?

ELESIN: In a night which falls before our eyes
               However deep, we do not miss our way.

PRAISE-SINGER: Shall I now not acknowledge I have stood
               Where wonders met their end? The elephant
                  deserves
               Better than that we say 'I have caught
               A glimpse of something'. If we see the tamer
               Of the forest let us say plainly, we have seen
               An elephant.

ELESIN (his voice is drowsy):
               I have freed myself of earth and now
               It's getting dark. Strange voices guide my feet.

PRAISE-SINGER: The river is never so high that the eyes
               Of a fish are covered. The night is not so dark
               That the albino fails to find his way. A child
               Returning homewards craves no leading by
                  the hand.
               Gracefully does the mask regain his grove at
                  the end of day . . .
               Gracefully. Gracefully does the mask dance
               Homeward at the end of day, gracefully . . .

(ELESIN's trance appears to be deepening, his steps heavier.)

IYALOJA: It is the death of war that kills the valiant,
               Death of water is how the swimmer goes
               It is the death of markets that kills the
                  trader
               And death of indecision takes the idle away
               The trade of the cutlass blunts its edge
               And the beautiful die the death of beauty.
               It takes an Elesin to die the death of death . . .
               Only Elesin . . . dies the unknowable death
                  of death . . .
               Gracefully, gracefully does the horseman
                  regain
               The stables at the end of day, gracefully . . .

PRAISE-SINGER: How shall I tell what my eyes have seen? The
   Horseman gallops on before the courier, how shall I tell what
   my eyes have seen? He says a dog may be confused by new

scents of beings he never dreamt of, so he must precede the dog to heaven. He says a horse may stumble on strange boulders and be lamed, so he races on before the horse to heaven. It is best, he says, to trust no messenger who may falter at the outer gate; oh how shall I tell what my ears have heard? But do you hear me still Elesin, do you hear your faithful one?

(ELESIN in his motions appear to feel for a direction of sound, subtly, but he only sinks deeper into his trance-dance.)

Elesin Alafin, I no longer sense your flesh. The drums are changing now but you have gone far ahead of the world. It is not yet noon in heaven; let those who claim it is begin their own journey home. So why must you rush like an impatient bride: why do you race to desert your Olohun-iyo?

(ELESIN is now sunk fully deep in his trance, there is no longer sign of any awareness of his surroundings.)

Does the deep voice of *gbedu* cover you then, like the passage of royal elephants? Those drums that brook no rivals, have they blocked the passage to your ears that my voice passes into wind, a mere leaf floating in the night? Is your flesh lightened Elesin, is that lump of earth I slid between your slippers to keep you longer slowly sifting from your feet? Are the drums on the other side now tuning skin to skin with ours in *osugbo*? Are there sounds there I cannot hear, do footsteps surround you which pound the earth like *gbedu*, roll like thunder round the dome of the world? Is the darkness gathering in your head Elesin? Is there now a streak of light at the end of the passage, a light I dare not look upon? Does it reveal whose voices we often heard, whose touches we often felt, whose wisdoms come suddenly into the mind when the wisest have shaken their heads and murmured; It cannot be done? Elesin Alafin, don't think I do not know why your lips are heavy, why your limbs are drowsy as palm oil in the cold of harmattan. I would call you back but when the elephant heads for the jungle, the tail is too small a handhold for the hunter that would pull him back. The sun that heads for the sea no longer heeds the prayers of the farmer. When the river begins to taste the salt of the ocean, we no longer know what deity to call on, the river-god or Olokun. No arrow flies back to the string, the child does not return through the same passage that gave it birth. Elesin Oba, can you hear me at all? Your eyelids are glazed like a courtesan's, is it that you see the dark groom and master of life? And will you see my father? Will you tell him that I stayed with you to the last? Will my voice ring in your ears awhile, will you remember Olohun-iyo even if the music on the other side surpasses his mortal craft? But will they know you over there? Have they eyes to gauge your worth, have they the heart to love you, will they know what thoroughbred prances towards them in caparisons of honour? If they do not Elesin, if any there cuts your yam with a small knife, or pours you wine in a small calabash, turn back and return to welcoming hands. If the world were not greater than the wishes of Olohun-iyo, I would not let you go . . .

(He appears to break down. ELESIN dances on, completely in a trance. The dirge wells up louder and stronger. ELESIN's dance does not lose its elasticity but his gestures become, if possible, even more weighty. Lights fade slowly on the scene.)

4

A Masque. The front side of the stage is part of a wide corridor around the great hall of the Residency extending beyond vision into the rear and wings. It is redolent of the tawdry decadence of a far-flung but key imperial frontier. The couples in a variety of fancy-dress are ranged around the walls, gazing in the same direction. The guest-of-honour is about to make an appearance. A portion of the local police brass band with its white conductor is just visible. At last, the entrance of Royalty. The band plays 'Rule Britannia', badly, beginning long before he is visible. The couples bow and curtsey as he passes by them. Both he and his companions are dressed in seventeenth century European costume. Following behind are the RESIDENT and his partner similarly attired. As they gain the end of the hall where the orchestra dais begins the music comes to an end. The PRINCE bows to the guests. The band strikes up a Viennese waltz and the PRINCE formally opens the floor. Several bars later the

RESIDENT and his companion follow suit. Others follow in appropriate pecking order. The orchestra's waltz rendition is not of the highest musical standard.

Some time later the PRINCE dances again into view and is settled into a corner by the RESIDENT who then proceeds to select couples as they dance past for introduction, sometimes threading his way through the dancers to tap the lucky couple on the shoulder. Desperate efforts from many to ensure that they are recognised in spite of, perhaps, their costume. The ritual of introductions soon takes in PILKINGS and his wife. The PRINCE is quite fascinated by their costume and they demonstrate the adaptations they have made to it, pulling down the mask to demonstrate how the *egungun* normally appears, then showing the various press-button controls they have innovated for the face flaps, the sleeves, etc. They demonstrate the dance steps and the guttural sounds made by the *egungun*, harrass other dancers in the hall, MRS PILKINGS playing the 'restrainer' to PILKINGS' manic darts. Everyone is highly entertained, the Royal Party especially who lead the applause.

At this point a liveried footman comes in with a note on a salver and is intercepted almost absent-mindedly by the RESIDENT who takes the note and reads it. After polite coughs he succeeds in excusing the PILKINGSES from the PRINCE and takes them aside. The PRINCE considerately offers the RESIDENT's wife his hand and dancing is resumed.

On their way out the RESIDENT gives an order to his AIDE-DE-CAMP. They come into the side corridor where the RESIDENT hands the note to PILKINGS.

RESIDENT: As you see it says 'emergency' on the outside. I took the liberty of opening it because His Highness was obviously enjoying the entertainment. I didn't want to interrupt unless really necessary.

PILKINGS: Yes, yes of course sir.

RESIDENT: Is it really as bad as it says? What's it all about?

PILKINGS: Some strange custom they have sir. It seems because the King is dead some important chief has to commit suicide.

RESIDENT: The King? Isn't it the same one who died nearly a month ago?

PILKINGS: Yes sir.

RESIDENT: Haven't they buried him yet?

PILKINGS: They take their time about these things sir. The pre-burial ceremonies last nearly thirty days. It seems tonight is the final night.

RESIDENT: But what has it got to do with the market women? Why are they rioting? We've waived that troublesome tax haven't we?

PILKINGS: We don't quite know that they are exactly rioting yet sir. Sergeant Amusa is sometimes prone to exaggerations.

RESIDENT: He sounds desperate enough. That comes out even in his rather quaint grammar. Where is the man anyway? I asked my aide-de-camp to bring him here.

PILKINGS: They are probably looking in the wrong verandah. I'll fetch him myself.

RESIDENT: No no you stay here. Let your wife go and look for them. Do you mind my dear . . . ?

JANE: Certainly not, your Excellency. (Goes.)

RESIDENT: You should have kept me informed Pilkings. You realise how disastrous it would have been if things had erupted while His Highness was here.

PILKINGS: I wasn't aware of the whole business until tonight sir.

RESIDENT: Nose to the ground Pilkings, nose to the ground. If we all let these little things slip past us where would the empire be eh? Tell me that. Where would we all be?

PILKINGS (low voice): Sleeping peacefully at home I bet.

RESIDENT: What did you say Pilkings?

PILKINGS: It won't happen again sir.

RESIDENT: It mustn't Pilkings. It musn't. Where is that damned sergeant? I ought to get back to His Highness as quickly as possible and offer him some plausible explanation for my rather abrupt conduct. Can you think of one Pilkings?

PILKINGS: You could tell him the truth sir.

RESIDENT: I could? No no no no Pilkings, that would never do. What! Go and tell him there is a riot just two miles away from him? This is supposed to be a secure colony of His Majesty, Pilkings.

PILKINGS: Yes sir.

RESIDENT: Ah, there they are. No, these are not our native police. Are these the ring-leaders of the riot?

PILKINGS: Sir, these are my police officers.

RESIDENT: Oh, I beg your pardon officers. You do look a little . . . I say, isn't there something missing in their uniform? I think they used to have some rather colourful sashes. If I remember rightly I recommended them myself in my young days in the service. A bit of colour always appeals to the natives, yes, I remember putting that in my report. Well well well, where are we? Make your report man.

PILKINGS (moves close to AMUSA, between his teeth): And let's have no more superstitious nonsense from you Amusa or I'll throw you in the guardroom for a month and feed you pork!

RESIDENT: What's that? What has pork to do with it?

PILKINGS: Sir, I was just warning him to be brief. I'm sure you are most anxious to hear his report.

RESIDENT: Yes yes yes of course. Come on man, speak up. Hey, didn't we give them some colourful fez hats with all those wavy things, yes, pink tassells . . .

PILKINGS: Sir, I think if he was permitted to make his report we might find that he lost his hat in the riot.

RESIDENT: Ah yes indeed. I'd better tell His Highness that. Lost his hat in the riot, ha ha. He'll probably say well, as long as he didn't lose his head. (Chuckles to himself.) Don't forget to send me a report first thing in the morning young Pilkings.

PILKINGS: No sir.

RESIDENT: And whatever you do, don't let things get out of hand. Keep a cool head and - nose to the ground Pilkings. (Wanders off in the general direction of the hall.)

PILKINGS: Yes sir.

AIDE-DE-CAMP: Would you be needing me sir?

PILKINGS: No thanks Bob. I think His Excellency's need of you is greater than ours.

AIDE-DE-CAMP: We have a detachment of soldiers from the

capital sir. They accompanied His Highness up here.

PILKINGS: I doubt if it will come to that but, thanks, I'll bear it in mind. Oh, could you send an orderly with my cloak.

AIDE-DE-CAMP: Very good sir. (Goes.)

PILKINGS: Now Sergeant.

AMUSA: Sir . . . (Makes an effort, stops dead. Eyes to the ceiling.)

PILKINGS: Oh, not again.

AMUSA: I cannot against death to dead cult. This dress get power of dead.

PILKINGS: Alright, let's go. You are relieved of all further duty Amusa. Report to me first thing in the morning.

JANE: Shall I come Simon?

PILKINGS: No, there's no need for that. If I can get back later I will. Otherwise get Bob to bring you home.

JANE: Be careful Simon . . . I mean, be clever.

PILKINGS: Sure I will. You two, come with me. (As he turns to go, the clock in the Residency begins to chime. PILKINGS looks at his watch then turns, horror-stricken, to stare at his wife. The same thought clearly occurs to her. He swallows hard. An orderly brings his cloak.) It's midnight. I had no idea it was that late.

JANE: But surely . . . they don't count the hours the way we do. The moon, or something . . .

PILKINGS: I am . . . not so sure.

(He turns and breaks into a sudden run. The two constables follow, also at a run. AMUSA, who has kept his eyes on the ceiling throughout waits until the last of the footsteps has faded out of hearing. He salutes suddenly, but without once looking in the direction of the woman.)

AMUSA: Goodnight madam.

JANE: Oh. (She hesitates.) Amusa . . . (He goes off without seeming to have heard.) Poor Simon . . . (A figure emerges from the shadows, a young black man dressed in a sober western suit. He peeps into the hall, trying to make out the figures of the dancers.)

Who is that?

OLUNDE (emerging into the light): I didn't mean to startle you madam. I am looking for the District Officer.

JANE: Wait a minute . . . don't I know you? Yes, you are Olunde, the young man who . . .

OLUNDE: Mrs Pilkings! How fortunate. I came here to look for your husband.

JANE: Olunde! Let's look at you. What a fine young man you've become. Grand but solemn. Good God, when did you return? Simon never said a word. But you do look well Olunde. Really!

OLUNDE: You are . . . well, you look quite well yourself Mrs Pilkings. From what little I can see of you.

JANE: Oh, this. It's caused quite a stir I assure you, and not all of it very pleasant. You are not shocked I hope?

OLUNDE: Why should I be? But don't you find it rather hot in there? Your skin must find it difficult to breathe.

JANE: Well, it is a little hot I must confess, but it's all in a good cause.

OLUNDE: What cause Mrs Pilkings?

JANE: All this. The ball. And His Highness being here in person and all that.

OLUNDE (mildly): And that is the good cause for which you desecrate an ancestral mask?

JANE: Oh, so you are shocked after all. How disappointing.

OLUNDE: No I am not shocked Mrs Pilkings. You forget that I have now spent four years among your people. I discovered that you have no respect for what you do not understand.

JANE: Oh. So you've returned with a chip on your shoulder. That's a pity Olunde. I am sorry.

(An uncomfortable silence follows.)

I take it then that you did not find your stay in England altogether edifying.

OLUNDE: I don't say that. I found your people quite admirable in many ways, their conduct and courage in this war for instance.

50

JANE: Ah yes the war. Here of course it is all rather remote. From time to time we have a black-out drill just to remind us that there is a war on. And the rare convoy passes through on its way somewhere or on manoeuvres. Mind you there is the occasional bit of excitement like that ship that was blown up in the harbour.

OLUNDE: Here? Do you mean through enemy action?

JANE: Oh no, the war hasn't come that close. The captain did it himself. I don't quite understand it really. Simon tried to explain. The ship had to be blown up because it had become dangerous to the other ships, even to the city itself. Hundreds of the coastal population would have died.

OLUNDE: Maybe it was loaded with ammunition and had caught fire. Or some of those lethal gases they've been experimenting on.

JANE: Something like that. The captain blew himself up with it. Deliberately. Simon said someone had to remain on board to light the fuse.

OLUNDE: It must have been a very short fuse.

JANE (shrugs): I don't know much about it. Only that there was no other way to save lives. No time to devise anything else. The captain took the decision and carried it out.

OLUNDE: Yes . . . I quite believe it. I met men like that in England.

JANE: Oh just look at me! Fancy welcoming you back with such morbid news. Stale too. It was at least six months ago.

OLUNDE: I don't find it morbid at all. I find it rather inspiring. It is an affirmative commentary on life.

JANE: What is?

OLUNDE: That captain's self-sacrifice.

JANE: Nonsense. Life should never be thrown deliberately away.

OLUNDE: And the innocent people round the harbour?

JANE: Oh, how does one know? The whole thing was probably exaggerated anyway.

OLUNDE: That was a risk the captain couldn't take. But please Mrs Pilkings, do you think you could find your husband for me? I have to talk to him.

JANE: Simon? Oh. (As she recollects for the first time the full significance of OLUNDE's presence.) Simon is . . . there is a little problem in town. He was sent for. But . . . when did you arrive? Does Simon know you're here?

OLUNDE (suddenly earnest): I need your help Mrs Pilkings. I've always found you somewhat more understanding than your husband. Please find him for me and when you do, you must help me talk to him.

JANE: I'm afraid I don't quite . . . follow you. Have you seen my husband already?

OLUNDE: I went to your house. Your houseboy told me you were here. (He smiles.) He even told me how I would recognise you and Mr Pilkings.

JANE: Then you must know what my husband is trying to do for you.

OLUNDE: For me?

JANE: For you. For your people. And to think he didn't even know you were coming back! But how do you happen to be here? Only this evening we were talking about you. We thought you were still four thousand miles away.

OLUNDE: I was sent a cable.

JANE: A cable? Who did? Simon? The business of your father didn't begin till tonight.

OLUNDE: A relation sent it weeks ago, and it said nothing about my father. All it said was, Our King is dead. But I knew I had to return home at once so as to bury my father. I understood that.

JANE: Well, thank God you don't have to go through that agony. Simon is going to stop it.

OLUNDE: That's why I want to see him. He's wasting his time. And since he has been so helpful to me I don't want him to incur the enmity of our people. Especially over nothing.

JANE (sits down open-mouthed): You . . . you Olunde!

OLUNDE: Mrs Pilkings, I came home to bury my father. As soon as I heard the news I booked my passage home. In fact we were fortunate. We travelled in the same convoy as your Prince, so we had excellent protection.

JANE: But you don't think your father is also entitled to what-ever protection is available to him?

OLUNDE: How can I make you understand? He *has* protection. No one can undertake what he does tonight without the deepest protection the mind can conceive. What can you offer him in place of his peace of mind, in place of the honour and veneration of his own people? What would you think of your Prince if he had refused to accept the risk of losing his life on this voyage? This . . . showing-the-flag tour of colonial possessions.

JANE: I see. So it isn't just medicine you studied in England.

OLUNDE: Yet another error into which your people fall. You believe that everything which appears to make sense was learnt from you.

JANE: Not so fast Olunde. You have learnt to argue I can tell that, but I never said you made sense. However cleverly you try to put it, it is still a barbaric custom. It is even worse - it's feudal! The king dies and a chieftain must be buried with him. How feudalistic can you get!

OLUNDE (waves his hand towards the background. The PRINCE is dancing past again - to a different step - and all the guests are bowing and curtseying as he passes): And this? Even in the midst of a devastating war, look at that. What name would you give to that?

JANE: Therapy, British style. The preservation of sanity in the midst of chaos.

OLUNDE: Others would call it decadence. However, it doesn't really interest me. You white races know how to survive; I've seen proof of that. By all logical and natural laws this war should end with all the white races wiping out one another, wiping out their so-called civilisation for all time and reverting to a state of primitivism the like of which has so far only existed in your imagination when you thought of us. I thought all that at the beginning. Then I slowly realised that your greatest art is the art of survival. But at least have the humility to let others survive in their own way.

JANE: Through ritual suicide?

OLUNDE: Is that worse than mass suicide? Mrs Pilkings, what

do you call what those young men are sent to do by their generals in this war? Of course you have also mastered the art of calling things by names which don't remotely describe them.

JANE: You talk! You people with your long-winded, roundabout way of making conversation.

OLUNDE: Mrs Pilkings, whatever we do, we never suggest that a thing is the opposite of what it really is. In your newsreels I heard defeats, thorough, murderous defeats described as strategic victories. No wait, it wasn't just on your newsreels. Don't forget I was attached to hospitals all the time. Hordes of your wounded passed through those wards. I spoke to them. I spent long evenings by their bedside while they spoke terrible truths of the realities of that war. I know now how history is made.

JANE: But surely, in a war of this nature, for the morale of the nation you must expect . . .

OLUNDE: That a disaster beyond human reckoning be spoken of as a triumph? No. I mean, is there no mourning in the home of the bereaved that such blasphemy is permitted?

JANE (after a moment's pause): Perhaps I can understand you now. The time we picked for you was not really one for seeing us at our best.

OLUNDE: Don't think it was just the war. Before that even started I had plenty of time to study your people. I saw nothing, finally, that gave you the right to pass judgement on other peoples and their ways. Nothing at all.

JANE (hesitantly): Was it the . . . colour thing? I know there is some discrimination.

OLUNDE: Don't make it so simple, Mrs Pilkings. You make it sound as if when I left, I took nothing at all with me.

JANE: Yes . . . and to tell the truth, only this evening, Simon and I agreed that we never really knew what you left with.

OLUNDE: Neither did I. But I found out over there. I am grateful to your country for that. And I will never give it up.

JANE: Olunde, please , . . promise me something. Whatever you do, don't throw away what you have started to do. You want to be a doctor. My husband and I believe you will make an excellent one, sympathetic and competent. Don't let anything make you throw away your training.

OLUNDE (genuinely surprised): Of course not. What a strange idea. I intend to return and complete my training. Once the burial of my father is over.

JANE: Oh, please . . . !

OLUNDE: Listen! Come outside. You can't hear anything against that music.

JANE: What is it?

OLUNDE: The drums. Can you hear the change? Listen.

(The drums come over, still distant but more distinct. There is a change of rhythm, it rises to a crescendo and then, suddenly, it is cut off. After a silence, a new beat begins, slow and resonant.)

There. It's all over.

JANE: You mean he's . . .

OLUNDE: Yes Mrs Pilkings, my father is dead. His will-power has always been enormous; I know he is dead.

JANE (screams): How can you be so calllous! So unfeeling! You announce your father's own death like a surgeon looking down on some strange . . . stranger's body! You're just a savage like all the rest.

AIDE-DE-CAMP (rushing out): Mrs Pilkings. Mrs Pilkings. (She breaks down, sobbing.) Are you alright, Mrs Pilkings?

OLUNDE: She'll be alright. (Turns to go.)

AIDE-DE-CAMP: Who are you? And who the hell asked your opinion?

OLUNDE: You're quite right, nobody. (Going.)

AIDE-DE-CAMP: What the hell! Did you hear me ask you who you were?

OLUNDE: I have business to attend to.

AIDE-DE-CAMP: I'll give you business in a moment you impudent nigger. Answer my question!

OLUNDE: I have a funeral to arrange. Excuse me. (Going.)

AIDE-DE-CAMP: I said stop! Orderly!

JANE: No no, don't do that. I'm alright. And for heaven's sake don't act so foolishly. He's a family friend.

AIDE-DE-CAMP: Well he'd better learn to answer civil questions when he's asked them. These natives put a suit on and they get high opinions of themselves.

OLUNDE: Can I go now?

JANE: No no don't go. I must talk to you. I'm sorry about what I said.

OLUNDE: It's nothing Mrs Pilkings. And I'm really anxious to go. I couldn't see my father before, it's forbidden for me, his heir and successor to set eyes on him from the moment of the king's death. But now . . . I would like to touch his body while it is still warm.

JANE: You will. I promise I shan't keep you long. Only, I couldn't possibly let you go like that. Bob, please excuse us.

AIDE-DE-CAMP: If you're sure . . .

JANE: Of course I'm sure. Something happened to upset me just then, but I'm alright now. Really.

(The AIDE-DE-CAMP goes, somewhat reluctantly.)

OLUNDE: I mustn't stay long.

JANE: Please, I promise not to keep you. It's just that . . . oh you saw yourself what happens to one in this place. The Resident's man thought he was being helpful, that's the way we all react. But I can't go in among that crowd just now and if I stay by myself somebody will come looking for me. Please, just say something for a few moments and then you can go. Just so I can recover myself.

OLUNDE: What do you want me to say?

JANE: Your calm acceptance for instance, can you explain that? It was so unnatural. I don't understand that at all. I feel a need to understand all I can.

OLUNDE: But you explained it yourself. My medical training perhaps. I have seen death too often. And the soldiers who returned from the front, they died on our hands all the time.

JANE: No. It has to be more than that. I feel it has to do with the many things we don't really grasp about your people. At least you can explain.

OLUNDE: All these things are part of it. And anyway, my father has been dead in my mind for nearly a month. Ever since I learnt of the King's death. I've lived with my bereavement so long now that I cannot think of him alive. On that journey on the boat, I kept my mind on my duties as the one who must perform the rites over his body. I went through it all again and again in my mind as he himself had taught me. I didn't want to do anything wrong, something which might jeopardise the welfare of my people.

JANE: But he had disowned you. When you left he swore publicly you were no longer his son.

OLUNDE: I told you, he was a man of tremendous will. Sometimes that's another way of saying stubborn. But among our people, you don't disown a child just like that. Even if I had died before him I would still be buried like his eldest son. But it's time for me to go.

JANE: Thank you. I feel calmer. Don't let me keep you from your duties.

OLUNDE: Goodnight Mrs Pilkings.

JANE: Welcome home. (She holds out her hand. As he takes it footsteps are heard approaching the drive. A short while later a woman's sobbing is also heard.)

PILKINGS (off): Keep them here till I get back. (He strides into view, reacts at the sight of OLUNDE but turns to his wife.) Thank goodness you're still here.

JANE: Simon, what happened?

PILKINGS: Later Jane, please. Is Bob still here?

JANE: Yes, I think so. I'm sure he must be.

PILKINGS: Try and get him out here as quietly as you can. Tell him it's urgent.

JANE: Of course. Oh Simon, you remember . . .

PILKINGS: Yes yes. I can see who it is. Get Bob out here. (She runs off.) At first I thought I was seeing a ghost.

OLUNDE: Mr Pilkings, I appreciate what you tried to do. I want you to believe that. I can only tell you it would have been a terrible calamity if you'd succeeded.

PILKINGS (opens his mouth several times, shuts it): You . . . said what?

OLUNDE: A calamity for us, the entire people.

PILKINGS (sighs): I see. Hm.

OLUNDE: And now I must go. I must see him before he turns cold.

PILKINGS: Oh ah . . . em . . . but this is a shock to see you. I mean er thinking all this while you were in England and thanking God for that.

OLUNDE: I came on the mail boat. We travelled in the Prince's convoy.

PILKINGS: Ah yes, a-ah, hm . . . er well . . .

OLUNDE: Goodnight. I can see you are shocked by the whole business. But you must know by now there are things you cannot understand - or help.

PILKINGS: Yes. Just a minute. There are armed policemen that way and they have instructions to let no one pass. I suggest you wait a little. I'll er . . . yes, I'll give you an escort.

OLUNDE: That's very kind of you. But do you think it could be quickly arranged.

PILKINGS: Of course. In fact, yes, what I'll do is send Bob over with some men to the er . . . place. You can go with them. Here he comes now. Excuse me a minute.

AIDE-DE-CAMP: Anything wrong sir?

PILKINGS (takes him to one side): Listen Bob, that cellar in the disused annexe of the Residency, you know, where the slaves were stored before being taken down to the coast . . .

AIDE-DE-CAMP: Oh yes, we use it as a storeroom for broken furniture.

PILKINGS: But it's still got the bars on it?

AIDE-DE-CAMP: Oh yes, they are quite intact.

PILKINGS: Get the keys please. I'll explain later. And I want a strong guard over the Residency tonight.

AIDE-DE-CAMP: We have that already. The detachment from the coast . . .

PILKINGS: No, I don't want them at the gates of the Residency. I want you to deploy them at the bottom of the hill, a long way from the main hall so they can deal with any situation long before the sound carries to the house.

AIDE-DE-CAMP: Yes of course.

PILKINGS: I don't want His Highness alarmed.

AIDE-DE-CAMP: You think the riot will spread here?

PILKINGS: It's unlikely but I don't want to take a chance. I made them believe I was going to lock the man up in my house, which was what I had planned to do in the first place. They are probably assailing it by now. I took a roundabout route here so I don't think there is any danger at all. At least not before dawn. Nobody is to leave the premises of course - the native employees I mean. They'll soon smell something is up and they can't keep their mouths shut.

AIDE-DE-CAMP: I'll give instructions at once.

PILKINGS: I'll take the prisoner down myself. Two policemen will stay with him throughout the night. Inside the cell.

AIDE-DE-CAMP: Right sir. (Salutes and goes off at the double.)

PILKINGS: Jane. Bob is coming back in a moment with a detachment. Until he gets back please stay with Olunde. (He makes an extra warning gesture with his eyes.)

OLUNDE: Please Mr Pilkings . . .

PILKINGS: I hate to be stuffy old son, but we have a crisis on our hands. It has to do with your father's affair if you must know. And it happens also at a time when we have His Highness here. I am responsible for security so you'll simply have to do as I say. I hope that's understood. (Marches off quickly, in the direction from which he made his first appearance.)

OLUNDE: What's going on? All this can't be just because he failed to stop my father killing himself.

JANE: I honestly don't know. Could it have sparked off a riot?

OLUNDE: No. If he'd succeeded that would be more likely to start the riot. Perhaps there were other factors involved. Was there a chieftancy dispute?

JANE: None that I know of.

ELESIN (an animal bellow from off): Leave me alone! Is it not enough that you have covered me in shame! White man, take your hand from my body!

(OLUNDE stands frozen on the spot. JANE understanding at last, tries to move him.)

JANE: Let's go in. It's getting chilly out here.

PILKINGS (off): Carry him.

ELESIN: Give me back the name you have taken away from me you ghost from the land of the nameless!

PILKINGS: Carry him! I can't have a disturbance here. Quickly! stuff up his mouth.

JANE: Oh God! Let's go in. Please Olunde. (OLUNDE does not move.)

ELESIN: Take your albino's hand from me you . . .

(Sounds of a struggle. His voice chokes as he is gagged.)

OLUNDE (quietly): That was my father's voice.

JANE: Oh you poor orphan, what have you come home to?

(There is a sudden explosion of rage from off-stage and powerful steps come running up the drive.)

PILKINGS: You bloody fools, after him!

(Immediately ELESIN, in handcuffs, comes pounding in the direction of JANE and OLUNDE, followed some moments afterwards by PILKINGS and the constables. ELESIN confronted by the seeming statue of his son, stops dead. OLUNDE stares above his head into the distance. The constables try to grab him. JANE screams at them.)

JANE: Leave him alone! Simon, tell them to leave him alone.

PILKINGS: All right, stand aside you. (Shrugs.) Maybe just as well. It might help to calm him down.

(For several moments they hold the same position. ELESIN moves a few steps forward, almost as if he's still in doubt.)

ELESIN: Olunde? (He moves his head, inspecting him from side to side.) Olunde! (He collapses slowly at OLUNDE's feet.) Oh son, don't let the sight of your father turn you blind!

OLUNDE (he moves for the first time since he heard his voice, brings his head slowly down to look on him): I have no father, eater of left-overs.

(He walks slowly down the way his father had run. Light fades out on ELESIN, sobbing into the ground.)

5

A wide iron-barred gate stretches almost the whole width of the cell in which ELESIN is imprisoned. His wrists are encased in thick iron bracelets, chained together; he stands against the bars, looking out. Seated on the ground to one side on the outside is his recent bride, her eyes bent perpetually to the ground. Figures of the two guards can be seen deeper inside the cell, alert to every movement ELESIN makes. PILKINGS now in a police officer's uniform enters noiselessly, observes him for a while. Then he coughs ostentatiously and approaches. Leans against the bars near a corner, his back to ELESIN. He is obviously trying to fall in mood with him. Some moments' silence.

PILKINGS: You seem fascinated by the moon.

ELESIN (after a pause): Yes, ghostly one. Your twin-brother up there engages my thoughts.

PILKINGS: It is a beautiful night.

ELESIN: Is that so?

PILKINGS: The light on the leaves, the peace of the night . . .

ELESIN: The night is not at peace, District Officer.

PILKINGS: No? I would have said it was. You know, quiet . . .

ELESIN: And does quiet mean peace for you?

PILKINGS: Well, nearly the same thing. Naturally there is a subtle difference . . .

ELESIN: The night is not at peace ghostly one. The world is not at peace. You have shattered the peace of the world for ever. There is no sleep in the world tonight.

PILKINGS: It is still a good bargain if the world should lose one night's sleep as the price of saving a man's life.

ELESIN: You did not save my life District Officer. You destroyed it.

PILKINGS: Now come on . . .

ELESIN: And not merely my life but the lives of many. The end of the night's work is not over. Neither this year nor the next will see it. If I wished you well, I would pray that you do not stay long enough on our land to see the disaster you have brought upon us.

PILKINGS: Well, I did my duty as I saw it. I have no regrets.

ELESIN: No. The regrets of life always come later.

(Some moments' pause.)

You are waiting for dawn white man. I hear you saying to yourself: only so many hours until dawn and then the danger is over. All I must do is keep him alive tonight. You don't quite understand it all but you know that tonight is when what ought to be must be brought about. I shall ease your mind even more, ghostly one. It is not an entire night but a moment of the night, and that moment is past. The moon was my messenger and guide. When it reached a certain gateway in the sky, it touched that moment for which my whole life has been spent in blessings. Even I do not know the gateway. I have stood here and scanned the sky for a glimpse of that door but, I cannot see it. Human eyes are useless for a search of this nature. But in the house of *osugbo*, those who keep watch through the spirit recognised the moment, they sent word to me through the voice of our sacred drums to prepare myself. I heard them and I shed all thoughts of earth. I began to follow the moon to the abode of gods . . . servant of the white king, that was when you entered my chosen place of departure on feet of desecration.

PILKINGS: I'm sorry, but we all see our duty differently.

ELESIN: I no longer blame you. You stole from me my first-born, sent him to your country so you could turn him into something in your own image. Did you plan it all beforehand? There are moments when it seems part of a larger plan. He who must follow my footsteps is taken from me, sent across the ocean. Then, in my turn, I am stopped from fulfilling my destiny. Did you think it all out before, this plan to push our world from its course and sever the cord that links us to the great origin?

PILKINGS: You don't really believe that. Anwyay, if that was my intention with your son, I appear to have failed.

ELESIN: You did not fail in the main thing ghostly one. We know the roof covers the rafters, the cloth covers blemishes; who would have known that the white skin covered our future, preventing us from seeing the death our enemies had prepared for us. The world is set adrift and its inhabitants are lost. Around them, there is nothing but emptiness.

PILKINGS: Your son does not take so gloomy a view.

ELESIN: Are you dreaming now white man? Were you not present at my reunion of shame? Did you not see when the world reversed itself and the father fell before his son, asking forgiveness?

PILKINGS: That was in the heat of the moment. I spoke to him and . . . if you want to know, he wishes he could cut out his tongue for uttering the words he did.

ELESIN: No. What he said must never be unsaid. The contempt of my own son rescued something of my shame at your hands. You may have stopped me in my duty but I know now that I did give birth to a son. Once I mistrusted him for seeking the companionship of those my spirit knew as enemies of our race. Now I understand. One should seek to obtain the secrets of his enemies. He will avenge my shame, white one. His spirit will destroy you and yours.

PILKINGS: That kind of talk is hardly called for. If you don't want my consolation . . .

ELESIN: No white man, I do not want your consolation.

PILKINGS: As you wish. Your son anyway, sends his consolation. He asks your forgiveness. When I asked him not to despise you his reply was: I cannot judge him, and if I cannot judge him, I cannot despise him. He wants to come to you to say goodbye and to receive your blessing.

ELESIN: Goodbye? Is he returning to your land?

PILKINGS: Don't you think that's the most sensible thing for him to do? I advised him to leave at once, before dawn, and he agrees that is the right course of action.

ELESIN: Yes, it is best. And even if I did not think so, I have lost the father's place of honour. My voice is broken.

PILKINGS: Your son honours you. If he didn't he would not ask your blessing.

ELESIN: No. Even a thoroughbred is not without pity for the turf he strikes with his hoof. When is he coming?

PILKINGS: As soon as the town is a little quieter. I advised it.

ELESIN: Yes white man, I am sure you advised it. You advise all our lives although on the authority of what gods, I do not know.

PILKINGS (opnes his mouth to reply, then appears to change his mind. Turns to go. Hesitates and stops again): Before I leave you, may I ask just one thing of you?

ELESIN: I am listening.

PILKINGS: I wish to ask you to search the quiet of your heart and tell me - do you not find great contradictions in the wisdom of your own race?

ELESIN: Make yourself clear, white one.

PILKINGS: I have lived among you long enough to learn a saying or two. One came to my mind tonight when I stepped into the market and saw what was going on. You were surrounded by those who egged you on with song and praises. I thought, are these not the same people who say: the elder grimly approaches heaven and you ask him to bear your greetings yonder; do you really think he makes the journey willingly? After that, I did not hesitate.

(A pause. ELESIN sighs. Before he can speak a sound of running feet is heard.)

JANE (off): Simon! Simon!

PILKINGS: What on earth . . ! (Runs off.)

(ELESIN turns to his new wife, gazes on her for some moments.)

64

ELESIN: My young bride, did you hear the ghostly one? You sit and sob in your silent heart but say nothing to all this. First I blamed the white man, then I blamed my gods for deserting me. Now I feel I want to blame you for the mystery of the sapping of my will. But blame is a strange peace offering for a man to bring a world he has deeply wronged, and to its innocent dwellers. Oh little mother, I have taken countless women in my life but you were more than a desire of the flesh. I needed you as the abyss across which my body must be drawn, I filled it with earth and dropped my seed in it at the moment of preparedness for my crossing. You were the final gift of the living to their emissary to the land of the ancestors, and perhaps your warmth and youth brought new insights of this world to me and turned my feet leaden on this side of the abyss. For I confess to you, daughter, my weakness came not merely from the abomination of the white man who came violently into my fading presence, there was also a weight of longing on my earth-held limbs. I would have shaken it off, already my foot had begun to lift but then, the white ghost entered and all was defiled.

(Approaching voices of PILKINGS and his wife.)

JANE: Oh Simon, you will let her in won't you?

PILKINGS: I really wish you'd stop interfering.

(They come in view. JANE is in a dressing-gown. PILKINGS is holding a note to which he refers from time to time.)

JANE: Good gracious, I didn't initiate this. I was sleeping quietly, or trying to anyway, when the servant brought it. It's not my fault if one can't sleep undisturbed even in the Residency.

PILKINGS: He'd have done the same if we were sleeping at home so don't sidetrack the issue. He knows he can get round you or he wouldn't send you the petition in the first place.

JANE: Be fair Simon. After all he was thinking of your own interests. He is grateful you know, you seem to forget that. He feels he owes you something.

PILKINGS: I just wish they'd leave this man alone tonight, that's all.

JANE: Trust him Simon. He's pledged his word it will all go peacefully.

65

PILKINGS: Yes, and that's the other thing. I don't like being threatened.

JANE: Threatened? (Takes the note.) I didn't spot any threat.

PILKINGS: It's there. Veiled, but it's there. The only way to prevent serious rioting tomorrow - what a cheek!

JANE: I don't think he's threatening you Simon.

PILKINGS: He's picked up the idiom alright. Wouldn't surprise me if he's been mixing with commies or anarchists over there. The phrasing sounds too good to be true. Damn! If only the Prince hadn't picked this time for his visit.

JANE: Well, even so Simon, what have you got to lose? You don't want a riot on your hands, not with the Prince here.

PILKINGS (going up to ELESIN): Let's see what he has to say. Chief Elesin, there is yet another person who wants to see you. As she is not a next-of-kin I don't really feel obliged to let her in. But your son sent a note with her, so it's up to you.

ELESIN: I know who that must be. So she found out your hiding-place. Well, it was not difficult. My stench of shame is so strong, it requires no hunter's dog to follow it.

PILKINGS: If you don't want to see her, just say so and I'll send her packing.

ELESIN: Why should I not want to see her? Let her come. I have no more holes in my rag of shame. All is laid bare.

PILKINGS: I'll bring her in. (Goes off.)

JANE (hesitates, then goes to ELESIN): Please, try and understand. Everything my husband did was for the best.

ELESIN (he gives her a long strange stare, as if he is trying to understand who she is): You are the wife of the District Officer?

JANE: Yes. My name, is Jane.

ELESIN: That is my wife sitting down there. You notice how still and silent she sits? My business is with your husband.

(PILKINGS returns with IYALOJA.)

PILKINGS: Here she is. Now first I want your word of honour that you will try nothing foolish.

ELESIN: Honour? White one, did you say you wanted my word
of honour?

PILKINGS: I know you to be an honourable man. Give me your
word of honour you will receive nothing from her.

ELESIN: But I am sure you have searched her clothing as you
would never dare touch your own mother. And there are
these two lizards of yours who roll their eyes even when I
scratch.

PILKINGS: And I shall be sitting on that tree trunk watching
even how you blink. Just the same I want your word that
you will not let her pass anything to you.

ELESIN: You have my honour already. It is locked up in that
desk in which you will put away your report of this night's
events. Even the honour of my people you have taken already;
it is tied together with those papers of treachery which make
you masters in this land.

PILKINGS: Alright. I am trying to make things easy but if you
must bring in politics we'll have to do it the hard way.
Madam, I want you to remain along this line and move no
nearer to that cell door. Guards! (They spring to attention.)
If she moves beyond this point, blow your whistle. Come
on Jane. (They go off.)

IYALOJA: How boldly the lizard struts before the pigeon when
it was the eagle itself he promised us he would confront.

ELESIN: I don't ask you to take pity on me Iyaloja. You have
a message for me or you would not have come. Even if it is
the curses of the world, I shall listen,

IYALOJA: You made so bold with the servant of the white
king who took your side against death. I must tell your
brother chiefs when I return how bravely you waged war
against him. Especially with words.

ELESIN: I more than deserve your scorn.

IYALOJA (with sudden anger): I warned you, if you must leave
a seed behind, be sure it is not tainted with the curses of the
world. Who are you to open a new life when you dared not
open the door to a new existence? I say who are you to
make so bold? (The BRIDE sobs and IYALOJA notices her.
Her contempt noticeably increases as she turns back to

ELESIN.) Oh you self-vaunted stem of the plantain, how hollow it all proves. The pith is gone in the parent stem, so how will it prove with the new shoot? How will it go with that earth that bears it? Who are you to bring this abomination on us!

ELESIN: My powers deserted me. My charms, my spells, even my voice lacked strength when I made to summon the powers that would lead me over the last measure of earth into the land of the fleshless. You saw it, Iyaloja. You saw me struggle to retrieve my will from the power of the stranger whose shadow fell across the doorway and left me floundering and blundering in a maze I had never before encountered. My senses were numbed when the touch of cold iron came upon my wrists. I could do nothing to save myself.

IYALOJA: You have betrayed us. We fed your sweetmeats such as we hoped awaited you on the other side. But you said No, I must eat the world's left-overs. We said you were the hunter who brought the quarry down; to you belonged the vital portions of the game. No, you said, I am the hunter's dog and I shall eat the entrails of the game and the faeces of the hunter. We said you were the hunter returning home in triumph, a slain buffalo pressing down on his neck; you said wait, I first must turn up this cricket hole with my toes. We said yours was the doorway at which we first spy the tapper when he comes down from the tree, yours was the blessing of the twilight wine, the purl that brings night spirits out of doors to steal their portion before the light of day. We said yours was the body of wine whose burden shakes the tapper like a sudden gust on his perch. You said, No, I am content to lick the dregs from each calabash when the drinkers are done. We said, the dew on earth's surface was for you to wash your feet along the slopes of honour. You said No, I shall step in the vomit of cats and the droppings of mice; I shall fight them for the left-overs of the world.

ELESIN: Enough Iyaloja, enough.

IYALOJA: We called you leader and oh, how you led us on. What we have no intention of eating should not be held to the nose.

ELESIN: Enough, enough. My shame is heavy enough.

IYALOJA: Wait. I came with a burden.

ELESIN: You have more than discharged it.

IYALOJA: I wish I could pity you.

ELESIN: I need neither your pity nor the pity of the world. I need understanding. Even I need to understand. You were present at my defeat. You were part of the beginnings. You brought about the renewal of my tie to earth, you helped in the binding of the cord.

IYALOJA: I gave you warning. The river which fills up before our eyes does not sweep us away in its flood.

ELESIN: What were warnings beside the moist contact of living earth between my fingers? What were warnings beside the renewal of famished embers lodged eternally in the heart of man. But even that, even if it overwhelmed one with a thousandfold temptations to linger a little while, a man could overcome it. It is when the alien hand pollutes the source of will, when a stranger force of violence shatters the mind's calm resolution, this is when a man is made to commit the awful treachery of relief, commit in his thought the unspeakable blasphemy of seeing the hand of the gods in this alien rupture of his world. I know it was this thought that killed me, sapped my powers and turned me into an infant in the hands of unnamable strangers. I made to utter my spells anew but my tongue merely rattled in my mouth. I fingered hidden charms and the contact was damp; there was no spark left to sever the life-strings that should stretch from every finger-tip. My will was squelched in the spittle of an alien race, and all because I had committed this blasphemy of thought - that there might be the hand of the gods in a stranger's intervention.

IYALOJA: Explain it how you will, I hope it brings you peace of mind. The bush-rat fled his rightful cause, reached the market and set up a lamentation. 'Please save me!' - are these fitting words to hear from an ancestral mask? 'There's a wild beast at my heels' is not becoming language from a hunter.

ELESIN: May the world forgive me.

IYALOJA: I came with a burden I said. It approaches the gates which are so well guarded by those jackals whose spittle will from this day on be your food and drink. But first, tell me, you who were once Elesin Oba, tell me, you who know so well the cycle of the plantain: is it the parent shoot which withers to give sap to the younger or, does your wisdom see it running the other way?

ELESIN: I don't see your meaning Iyaloja?

IYALOJA: Did I ask you for a meaning? I asked a question. Whose trunk withers to give sap to the other? The parent shoot or the younger?

ELESIN: The parent.

IYALOJA: Ah. So you do know that. There are sights in this world which say different Elesin. There are some who choose to reverse this cycle of our being. Oh you emptied bark that the world once saluted for a pith-laden being, shall I tell you what the gods have claimed of you?

(In her agitation she steps beyond the line indicated by PILKINGS and the air is rent by piercing whistles. The two GUARDS also leap forward and place safe-guarding hands on ELESIN. IYALOJA stops, astonished. PILKINGS comes racing in, followed by JANE.)

PILKINGS: What is it? Did they try something?

GUARD: She stepped beyond the line.

ELESIN (in a broken voice): Let her alone. She meant no harm.

IYALOJA: Oh Elesin, see what you've become. Once you had no need to open your mouth in explanation because evil-smelling goats, itchy of hand and foot had lost their senses. And it was a brave man indeed who dared lay hands on you because Iyaloja stepped from one side of the earth onto another. Now look at the spectacle of your life. I grieve for you.

PILKINGS: I think you'd better leave. I doubt you have done him much good by coming here. I shall make sure you are not allowed to see him again. In any case we are moving him to a different place before dawn, so don't bother to come back.

IYALOJA: We foresaw that. Hence the burden I trudged here to lay beside your gates.

PILKINGS: What was that you said?

IYALOJA: Didn't our son explain? Ask that one. He knows

70

what it is. At least we hope the man we once knew as Elesin remembers the lesser oaths he need not break.

PILKINGS: Do you know what she is talking about?

ELESIN: Go to the gates, ghostly one. Whatever you find there, bring it to me.

IYALOJA: Not yet. It drags behind me on the slow, weary feet of women. Slow as it is Elesin, it has long overtaken you. It rides ahead of your laggard will.

PILKINGS: What is she saying now? Christ! Must your people forever speak in riddles?

ELESIN: It will come white man, it will come. Tell your men at the gates to let it through.

PILKINGS (dubiously): I'll have to see what it is.

IYALOJA: You will. (Passionately.) But this is one oath he cannot shirk. White one, you have a king here, a visitor from your land. We know of his presence here. Tell me, were he to die would you leave his spirit roaming restlessly on the surface of earth? Would you bury him here among those you consider less than human? In your land have you no ceremonies of the dead?

PILKINGS: Yes. But we don't make our chiefs commit suicide to keep him company.

IYALOJA: Child, I have not come to help your understanding. (Points to ELESIN.) This is the man whose weakened understanding holds us in bondage to you. But ask him if you wish. He knows the meaning of a king's passage; he was not born yesterday. He knows the peril to the race when our dead father, who goes as intermediary, waits and waits and knows he is betrayed. He knows when the narrow gate was opened and he knows it will not stay for laggards who drag their feet in dung and vomit, whose lips are reeking of the left-overs of lesser men. He knows he has condemned our king to wander in the void of evil with beings who are enemies of life.

PILKINGS: Yes er . . . but look here . . .

IYALOJA: What we ask is little enough. Let him release our King so he can ride on homewards alone. The messenger is on his way on the backs of women. Let him send word through the heart that is folded up within the bolt. It is the least of all his oaths, it is the easiest fulfilled.

(The AIDE-DE-CAMP runs in.)

PILKINGS: Bob?

AIDE-DE-CAMP: Sir, there's a group of women chanting up the hill.

PILKINGS (rounding on IYALOJA): If you people want trouble . . .

JANE: Simon, I think that's what Olunde referred to in his letter.

PILKINGS: He knows damned well I can't have a crowd here! Damn it, I explained the delicacy of my position to him. I think it's about time I got him out of town. Bob, send a car and two or three soldiers to bring him in. I think the sooner he takes his leave of his father and gets out the better.

IYALOJA: Save your labour white one. If it is the father of your prisoner you want, Olunde, he who until this night we knew as Elesin's son, he comes soon himself to take his leave. He has sent the women ahead, so let them in.

(PILKINGS remains undecided.)

AIDE-DE-CAMP: What do we do about the invasion? We can still stop them far from here.

PILKINGS: What do they look like?

AIDE-DE-CAMP: They're not many. And they seem quite peaceful.

PILKINGS: No men?

AIDE-DE-CAMP: Mm, two or three at the most.

JANE: Honestly, Simon, I'd trust Olunde. I don't think he'll deceive you about their intentions.

PILKINGS: He'd better not. Alright, let them in Bob. Warn them to control themselves. Then hurry Olunde here. Make sure he brings his baggage because I'm not returning him into town.

AIDE-DE-CAMP: Very good sir. (Goes.)

PILKINGS (to IYALOJA): I hope you understand that if anything goes wrong it will be on your head. My men have orders to shoot at the first sign of trouble.

IYALOJA: To prevent one death you will actually make other deaths? Ah, great is the wisdom of the white race. But have no fear. Your Prince will sleep peacefully. So at long last will ours. We will disturb you no further, servant of the white king. Just let Elesin fulfil his oath and we will retire home and pay homage to our King.

JANE: I believe her Simon, don't you?

PILKINGS: Maybe.

ELESIN: Have no fear ghostly one. I have a message to send my King and then you have nothing more to fear.

IYALOJA: Olunde would have done it. The chiefs asked him to speak the words but he said no, not while you lived.

ELESIN: Even from the depths to which my spirit has sunk, I find some joy that this little has been left to me.

(The women enter, intoning the dirge 'Alẹ lẹ lẹ' and swaying from side to side. On their shoulders is borne a longish object roughly like a cylindrical bolt, covered in cloth. They set it down on the spot where IYALOJA had stood earlier, and form a semi-circle round it. The PRAISE-SINGER and DRUMMER stand on the inside of the semi-circle but the drum is not used at all. The DRUMMER intones under the PRAISE-SINGER's invocations.)

PILKINGS (as they enter): What is *that*?

IYALOJA: The burden you have made white one, but we bring it in peace.

PILKINGS: I said *what* is it?

ELESIN: White man, you must let me out. I have a duty to perform.

PILKINGS: I most certainly will not.

ELESIN: There lies the courier of my King. Let me out so I can perform what is demanded of me.

PILKINGS: You'll do what you need to do from inside there or not at all. I've gone as far as I intend to with this business.

ELESIN: The worshipper who lights a candle in your church

to bear a message to his god bows his head and speaks in a whisper to the flame. Have I not seen it ghostly one? His voice does not ring out to the world. Mine are no words for anyone's ears. They are not words even for the bearers of this load. They are words I must speak secretly, even as my father whispered them in my ears and I in the ears of my first-born. I cannot shout them to the wind and the open night-sky.

JANE: Simon . . .

PILKINGS: Don't interfere. Please!

IYALOJA: They have slain the favourite horse of the king and slain his dog. They have borne them from pulse to pulse centre of the land receiving prayers for their king. But the rider has chosen to stay behind. Is it too much to ask that he speak his heart to heart of the waiting courier? (PILKINGS turns his back on her.) So be it. Elesin Oba, you see how even the mere leavings are denied you. (She gestures to the PRAISE-SINGER.)

PRAISE-SINGER: Elesin Oba! I call you by that name only this last time. Remember when I said, if you cannot come, tell my horse. (Pause.) What? I cannot hear you? I said, if you cannot come, whisper in the ears of my horse. Is your tongue severed from the roots Elesin? I can hear no response. I said, if there are boulders you cannot climb, mount my horse's back, this spotless black stallion, he'll bring you over them. (Pauses.) Elesin Oba, once you had a tongue that darted like a drummer's stick. I said, if you get lost my dog will track a path to me. My memory fails me but I think you replied: My feet have found the path, Alafin.

(The dirge rises and falls.)

I said at the last, if evil hands hold you back, just tell my horse there is weight on the hem of your smock. I dare not wait too long.

(The dirge rises and falls.)

There lies the swiftest ever messenger of a king, so set me free with the errand of your heart. There lie the head and heart of the favourite of the gods, whisper in his ears. Oh my companion, if you had followed when you should, we would not say that the horse preceded its rider. If you had

followed when it was time, we would not say the dog has
raced beyond and left his master behind. If you had raised
your will to cut the thread of life at the summons of the
drums, we would not say your mere shadow fell across the
gateway and took its owner's place at the banquet. But the
hunter, laden with a slain buffalo, stayed to root in the
cricket's hole with his toes. What now is left? If there is a
dearth of bats, the pigeon must serve us for the offering.
Speak the words over your shadow which must now serve in
your place.

ELESIN: I cannot approach. Take off the cloth. I shall speak
my message from heart to heart of silence.

IYALOJA (moves forward and removes the covering): Your
courier Elesin, cast your eyes on the favoured companion
of the King.

(Rolled up in the mat, his head and feet showing at either
end is the body of OLUNDE.)

There lies the honour of your household and of our race.
Because he could not bear to let honour fly out of doors,
he stopped it with his life. The son has proved the father
Elesin, and there is nothing left in your mouth to gnash but
infant gums.

PRAISE-SINGER: Elesin, we placed the reins of the world in
your hands yet you watched it plunge over the edge of the
bitter precipice. You sat with folded arms while evil strangers
tilted the world from its course and crashed it beyond the
edge of emptiness - you muttered, there is little that one
man can do, you left us floundering in a blind future. Your
heir has taken the burden on himself. What the end will be,
we are not gods to tell. But this young shoot has poured its
sap into the parent stalk, and we know this is not the way
of life. Our world is tumbling in the void of strangers, Elesin.

(ELESIN has stood rock-still, his knuckles taut on the bars,
his eyes glued to the body of his son. The stillness seizes and
paralyses everyone, including PILKINGS who has turned to
look. Suddenly ELESIN flings one arm round his neck, once,
and with the loop of the chain, strangles himself in a swift,
decisive pull. The guards rush forward to stop him but they
are only in time to let his body down. PILKINGS has leapt
to the door at the same time and struggles with the lock. He

rushes within, fumbles with the handcuffs and unlocks them, raises the body to a sitting position while he tries to give resuscitation. The women continue their dirge, unmoved by the sudden event.)

IYALOJA: Why do you strain yourself? Why do you labour at tasks for which no one, not even the man lying there would give you thanks? He is gone at last into the passage but oh, how late it all is. His son will feast on the meat and throw him bones. The passage is clogged with droppings from the King's stallion; he will arrive all stained in dung.

PILKINGS (in a tired voice): Was this what you wanted?

IYALOJA: No child, it is what you brought to be, you who play with strangers' lives, who even usurp the vestments of our dead, yet believe that the stain of death will not cling to you. The gods demanded only the old expired plantain but you cut down the sap-laden shoot to feed your pride. There is your board, filled to overflowing. Feast on it. (She screams at him suddenly, seeing that PILKINGS is about to close ELESIN's staring eyes.) Let him alone! However sunk he was in debt he is no pauper's carrion abandoned on the road. Since when have strangers donned clothes of indigo before the bereaved cries out his loss?

(She turns to the BRIDE who has remained motionless throughout.)

Child.

(The girl takes up a little earth, walks calmly into the cell and closes ELESIN's eyes. She then pours some earth over each eyelid and comes out again.)

Now forget the dead, forget even the living. Turn your mind only to the unborn.

(She goes off, accompanied by the BRIDE. The dirge rises in volume and the women continue their sway. Lights fade to a black-out.)

THE END

GLOSSARY

alari a rich, woven cloth, brightly coloured

egungun ancestral masquerade

etutu placatory rites or medicine

gbedu a deep-timbred royal drum

opele string of beads used in Ifa divination

osugbo secret 'executive' cult of the Yoruba; its meeting place

robo a delicacy made from crushed melon seeds, fried in tiny balls

sanyan a richly valued woven cloth

sigidi a squat, carved figure, endowed with the powers of an incubus